you & your
Suzuki **4x4**

you & your
Suzuki 4x4

Paul Guinness | *Buying, enjoying, maintaining, modifying*

First published in January 2005

A catalogue record for this book is available from the British Library

ISBN 1 84425 121 7

Library of Congress catalog card no. 2004112998

Published by Haynes Publishing, Sparkford,
Yeovil, Somerset, BA22 7JJ, UK

Tel: 01963 442030 Fax: 01963 440001
Int. tel: +44 1963 442030 Int. fax: +44 1963 440001
E-mail: sales@haynes.co.uk
Website: www.haynes.co.uk

Haynes North America, Inc.,
861 Lawrence Drive, Newbury Park,
California 91320, USA

Pagebuild by Glad Stockdale
Printed and bound in England by
J. H. Haynes & Co. Ltd, Sparkford

Contents

Acknowledgements

As a Suzuki 4x4 admirer of long-standing, writing this book has been a pleasure for me, as have all the telephone calls, correspondence and e-mails from fellow enthusiasts and colleagues who have been supportive and encouraging throughout.

Particular thanks are due to Frank Westworth, motoring editor, author and great friend, who has not only allowed me to use some of his own photographs in this book, but whose encouragement, humour and sheer enthusiasm at all times has been priceless. I'm also particularly grateful to Rowena Hoseason, former editor of *4x4 Mart* magazine, for her support throughout these last few months.

Suzuki enthusiast and fellow contributor to *4x4 Mart*, John Richardson, has provided me with some stunning off-road photography for use in the book – a huge help and a tribute to his skills as modifier extraordinaire! Thanks, John.

I'm also full of praise for Suzuki GB's press office, an extremely efficient set-up that has been providing me with test vehicles since 1987, the year I drove my first ever SJ410. Some of those many vehicles are shown throughout the book, all of them bringing back fond memories of writing for so many different magazines over the years.

Paul Guinness
December 2004

Introduction

Any company that becomes one of the world's most successful manufacturers of all-wheel-drive vehicles in the space of just three decades must be doing something right. In the case of Suzuki, they do a lot of things very right indeed. And the popularity of these vehicles (which built steadily through the 1980s, exploded in the '90s and is now increasing further in the 21st century), shows no sign of abating.

In fact, Suzuki 4x4s are more popular than ever. Current models such as the Jimny and Grand Vitara offer unrivalled value for money in today's market, while older models like the SJ and original-style Vitara are now highly sought-after second-hand, both as practical and economical road cars and as seriously capable off-road funsters.

Many Europeans laughed when they saw the Suzuki LJ80 for the first time in 1978. It was the tiniest 4x4 ever to go into mass production, and many pundits were struggling to imagine who would buy such a vehicle. But the LJ was just the start and once its successor, the SJ410, arrived in 1982, things were looking up for Suzuki. Here was an affordable, economical, cheap-to-run 4x4 that was no more expensive to buy than a very ordinary hatchback. Suzuki had created a whole new market, and buyers were never in short supply.

The eventual launch of the Vitara effectively started the 4x4 'lifestyle' scene, a sector of the market that has continued to grow ever since. Here, at last, was a trendy, fun-to-drive 4x4 which turned as many heads as any GTI and was a lot cheaper to insure. No wonder it continued to sell in such large numbers throughout the 1990s and beyond.

Motoring historians will always cite Jeep and Land Rover as being at the forefront of 4x4 development; these two marques, dating back to the 1940s, were effectively responsible for launching the idea of affordable all-wheel-drive utility vehicles, long before anybody else had seriously considered the notion.

Suzuki though, can surely take credit for creating two completely new 4x4 classes since then. First came the 'diminutive' 4x4 epitomised by the LJ, a vehicle which cost less than half the price of a Land Rover when it was launched. Then came the 'trendy, lifestyle' 4x4 that began with the Vitara and is now responsible for a massive proportion of new all-wheel drive sales throughout the world.

In this book, I have tried to give a clear and accurate account of the entire history, development and progress of Suzuki 4x4 models. It is a fascinating story and one which, remarkably, has never been told before in such depth. I have also set out to offer invaluable advice on buying and running a Suzuki 4x4, as well as a guide to what you can do with one once you have acquired it.

Suzukis remain among the most modified of all 4x4s. Whether that means a chrome-and-alloys Vitara for looking good on the street, or a massively lifted and uprated Jimny for off-road fun, these vehicles appeal to owners who want to make them their own. And there's no shortage of accessories and modifications out there for the keen enthusiast.

Despite Suzuki introducing increasingly upmarket versions of their 4x4s over the years, this remains a company determined to maintain its reputation for value and economy – their loyal band of admirers and enthusiasts who continue to support its products will make sure of that.

This book is a celebration of Suzuki's success and of the vehicles themselves. It is a practical guide too, essential for anybody who is either thinking of buying a Suzuki or who already has one parked on their driveway. Whichever category you fall into, I hope you enjoy what follows.

Your average compact Suzuki 4x4 has come a long way since those utilitarian days of the 1970s. The 2004 entry-level Jimny was a major step up from its woefully basic but enormously useful forebear, the LJ80. Despite the extra equipment and added refinement though, the 21st century offering has always offered superb value for money. *(Suzuki GB)*

Chapter One

Arrival of the LJ

Ask most people to think of a Suzuki 4x4 and they tend to come up with broadly similar answers. Most of them will mention the Vitara. Almost as many might talk about the SJ and Samurai, while those more familiar with later models will probably bring the Jimny and Grand Vitara into the conversation. Few though, will instantly think of the LJ series, the models that first established Suzuki in the off-road market throughout much of Europe.

We're going back to 1978, a time when Suzuki was better known for motorbikes outside Japan than for four-wheeled – let alone four-wheel-drive – machinery. We are also going back to a time when the market for new 4x4s was vastly smaller than it is now, in these early years of the 21st century. So, for a relatively

unknown car brand like Suzuki to launch a new range of all-wheel-drive utility vehicles on to an unsuspecting British and European public … well, it was a brave step, to say the least. It was a leap into the unknown, but it was based upon Suzuki's conviction that not only did they have a decent vehicle to sell, but that there was a market ready to buy it.

Suzuki wasn't new to the 4x4 scene in 1978. Indeed, development of their first LJ model had begun a full decade earlier, a vehicle that went on to become the

With its front screen folded flat and its canvas roof and doors removed, the first of the go-anywhere Suzukis was at its most basic in LJ80 guise. This particular version wasn't the greatest vehicle for coping with the British climate, though. *(Suzuki GB)*

The initial British-spec LJ range in its entirety: the LJ80, LJ80V Hard-top and LJ81 Pick-up. 'Three models offering the advantages of light weight and compact design', boasted Suzuki in 1979. *(Suzuki GB)*

550cc three-cylinder LJ50 in 1974. That's when exports to Australia – one of the world's biggest 4x4 markets – began, a full three years before the LJ50 was developed into the bigger-engined but bodily identical LJ80. The following year, 1978, was when Suzuki took the decision to bring the new four-cylinder LJ80 model to Europe.

It would have been easy to mock Suzuki's decision. Most Brits, for example, had never seen anything quite like the diminutive LJ before and to them, a 4x4 was a Land Rover; end of discussion. If you couldn't afford a new Land Rover, you went out and bought a second-hand Land Rover. That was it, that was the rugged side of 4x4 life in the UK back then. What did most buyers want with a tiny, young upstart from Japan anyway?

What indeed. But the decision-makers at Suzuki were a canny lot. They had seen a slight – but important – shift in 4x4 buyers' habits during the 1970s, with Japanese models like the Toyota Land Cruiser finally selling a few examples despite the incredible market

dominance of the products of Solihull. By the late '70s, Daihatsu had been launched in the UK, selling their basic but rugged F20 and F50 workhorses. The tide was slowly starting to turn – and Suzuki was determined to catch a wave as soon as possible.

Happily, the company saw a gap at the bottom end of the market and it was a gap that was surely crying out to be filled. Not every Land Rover buyer really needed a vehicle that big, that expensive, that powerful or that indestructible. Maybe, just maybe, there were some buyers who wanted a cheap and cheerful, cut-price alternative.

The theory was a sound one. It somehow seemed to make sense – even though there were critics suggesting that if there really was a market for such a vehicle, surely somebody else would have produced it already? But Suzuki weren't about to start listening to such sceptics, insisting instead, on going with their own corporate gut instinct. The decision to bring their cheap, basic and economical off-roader to the UK was made.

Value for money
The Suzuki LJ arrived in the UK towards the end of 1978 – complete with a 797cc, 41bhp four-cylinder overhead-

cam powerplant under its tiny bonnet. Perhaps predictably, many Land Rover fanatics chortled to themselves when they first caught sight of Suzuki's new arrival. If nothing else though, at least the LJ had value for money in its favour. This was, by any standards, a cheap vehicle, and it was, rather importantly, the very cheapest off-roader available in the UK.

Just how cheap are we talking? Well, let's jump ahead to 1981 for a moment, if only because the 4x4 market had expanded slightly by then – which makes comparisons between the little LJ and a handful of 'rivals' that much easier…

By that year, you could buy a soft-top LJ80 for £3,450 or a hard-top LJ80V for just a hundred pounds more. To put that in perspective, a Daihatsu F20 cost £5,342, an ARO 240 was £5,865, a Jeep CJ-7 was priced at £5,536 and a Land Rover Series III short-wheelbase Station Wagon was a whopping £7,319. You could buy two Suzukis for the price of one basic Land Rover, and still have enough left over for a package holiday in Majorca. (Or you could buy a whole trio of Suzuki LJs for the price of a single Range Rover – a comparison that is perhaps not particularly valid, but interesting nevertheless.)

In reality, of course, the little Suzuki LJ had no direct competition. The Daihatsu F20 was the closest thing to a rival, but was appreciably bigger in terms of both power and physical size. The Daihatsu was a genuine

Above: The LJ80V was arguably the most sensible of the range, with all the advantages of an enclosed bodyshell and the off-road prowess of the other versions. Lack of brake horsepower was compensated for by the LJ80V's amazingly light, 785kg kerb weight. *(Suzuki GB)*

Below: Now that looks fun! But, of course, with the front screen folded and nothing above your head, there would be a problem with sand getting in your eyes… *(Suzuki GB)*

cut-price alternative to a Land Rover, while the Suzuki was simply in a class of its own.

Upon its UK launch, the most basic of LJs – the LJ80 – cost a mere £2,900, at which price level there was nothing to touch it. As with any new idea though (no other company had thought of launching such a cheap and tiny 4x4 in the UK before, remember), the LJ had to put up with a barrage of abuse and mocking before some folk would take it seriously. After all, how could something so lacking in power be any good off-road? How could something so small cope with rough terrain? How could something so cheap last more than a few months when used and abused by farmers and foresters? How indeed.

Proof of the pudding

Let's be honest here and admit that the Suzuki LJ was not a massive hit in Britain. In fact, by the time it disappeared from Suzuki showrooms at the end of 1982, four years after it first took a bow, just 1,901 examples of the little LJ had been sold in the UK. That means an average of just 475 LJs a year found British buyers, so perhaps the model's critics really did have a point after all?

To dismiss the LJ in such a way though, is to do it a great disservice. For a start, let's not forget that the LJ80 really was starting from scratch. Not only was this the creation of a new 4x4 market segment, it was simultaneous with the launch of a small network of Suzuki car dealers and the introduction of the Suzuki marque to Britain's 'four-wheel' buyers. Looked at in those terms, even less than 500 LJ sales a year seems quite respectable.

Ironically, the LJ80 started to become more popular towards the end of its life in the UK. People in the market for an inexpensive and useful four-wheel-drive tool were beginning to warm to the Suzuki's charms. Also, after a couple of years on sale, as word of its actual competence began to spread, the humble LJ was quietly proving itself to be a hard worker.

Land Rover fans may have laughed initially at the idea of a 797cc engine powering a four-wheel-drive machine, but many were later eating their words when the LJ finally proved its worth. Unlike a Land Rover, the LJ80 was an ultra lightweight vehicle, tipping the scales at just 740kg for the basic soft-top version. This meant it was able to skip its way over the top of muddy situations which saw many heavier machines bogging down and becoming stuck. In fact, with the driver making full use of its high-revving overhead-cam 41bhp petrol engine, any LJ80 would tackle steep inclines, deep ruts, muddy tracks and generally rough terrain with surprising ease. It floated where others sank; it flew where others plodded, and it did it all with an eagerness and willingness that endeared it to its driver.

Not everything about the LJ80 off-road was fabulous, of course. For a start, a relatively high-revving petrol engine could not hope to offer the same kind of torque figures or the same levels of downhill engine braking as

The LJ81 light truck certainly had its uses – although with a maximum payload of just 250kg, carrying heavy weights around wasn't one of them! It nevertheless filled a useful niche in the 4x4 market that every other manufacturer seemed to be ignoring at the end of the 1970s.
(Suzuki GB)

a lower-revving diesel powerplant. So that was one major advantage of the likes of Land Rover, but unless you intended embarking upon some really serious off-road driving every day, this wouldn't necessarily be a major issue.

The LJ80's generally impressive off-road capabilities were not all down to its lack of weight, of course. A generous, 240mm of ground clearance was a great aid, and this was a technically competent machine too, setting a trend by having as standard a dual-range transfer box. On-road driving was predominantly rear-wheel drive, in all but the most severe conditions. Off-road though, a choice of high- or low-ratio all-wheel-drive gearing provided an ideal compromise for most situations. The LJ may have offered only a four-speed gearbox, but its dual-range transfer box at least made the most of it.

Above: With its rear-mounted spare wheel and square, boxy body, the LJ80V of 1979 was already setting a styling trend that would follow on through subsequent 'entry level' Suzukis − including the SJ of the 1980s and the Jimny of the '90s. *(Suzuki GB)*

Below: Just three derivatives of the LJ were on sale initially − and in a choice of just three colours, too. Whichever LJ model you opted for, it was offered in either Pastel Blue, Panama Red or the bizarrely named Francois White No. 2. *(Suzuki GB)*

Almost inevitably, the rest of the LJ's specification was both straightforward and basic. Its separate steel chassis was of conventional design and its leaf-sprung suspension performed its role adequately. This was long before coil springs and independent suspension started to play a major role in everyday 4x4s, with the obvious exception of the Range Rover, but with a price tag the

'Inside were some seats, three pedals, a heater, a steering wheel and, wait for it, wind-up windows on the steel doors. Surprisingly that last feature actually warranted a mention in Suzuki's advertising campaign of the day. At the time, Land Rover's Series III made do with sliding glass in its doors.'
(Rhino magazine, Winter 2003)

Above: Before the days of 4x4s being bought as fashion statements or for the daily school run, models like the humble LJ80V were marketed very much as workhorses. It was a role the LJ series performed impressively well. *(Suzuki GB)*

Right: 'Tough, square head-pipe steel is used to form the heart of the main frame', explained Suzuki in their efforts to describe the LJ's separate chassis. The trick was to keep the chassis as lightweight as possible, while endowing it with enough rigidity and strength to be effective off-road. The use of strengthening crossmembers was a logical answer. *(Suzuki GB)*

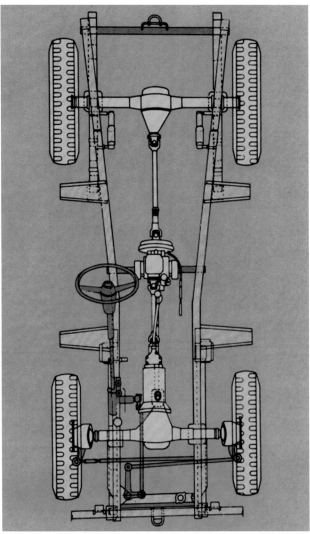

best part of £10,000 by the time the sub-£3k LJ80 went on sale, that is perhaps hardly surprising.

What the utilitarian Suzuki lacked in technological advances though, it more than made up for in reliability and durability. These machines soon became renowned for taking abuse in their stride and they seemed to thrive on a diet of hard work and neglect in many users' hands. They were mechanically robust, and that showed in the punishment they would happily take on a daily basis.

Sadly though, the mechanical longevity was not matched by the durability of the LJ80's bodywork, as despite its fairly sturdy chassis and simple body panel designs, the Suzuki LJ was quite a rust-prone machine. Arguably, its corrosion problems were no worse than the more conventional Japanese cars of the late 1970s, but in the 4x4 market, when compared with the likes of the predominantly aluminium-bodied Land Rover, it was something of a letdown.

The solution? This was to let the LJ80 became almost a 'throwaway tool'. It was so utterly cheap to buy, it was worth getting hold of one and simply running it into the ground. If the owner managed to get a fair few years of use out of it before scrapping it, that was all well and good.

No wonder then, that the vast majority of the 1,901 LJ80s sold in the UK have long since disappeared. Nobody bought an LJ to cherish or to pamper, and that certainly shows in today's survival figures.

Limited choice

Even when it was new, the LJ range was not a vast one. Upon its launch in 1978, just three versions were available, comprising the open-air LJ80, LJ80V hard-top and the LJ81K pick-up truck.

No LJ80 was ever a luxury machine, of course. In fact, the range gave a whole new meaning to the term 'basic', but really that was all part of the vehicle's charm

Above: So that's what they mean by water sports…? An early LJ80 demonstrates the model's wading capabilities – much to the delight of a rather sodden driver. *(Suzuki GB)*

Left: If you needed some kind of weather protection, your basic LJ80 came with canvas top and doors. Those tubular-framed doors offered zip-out windows for extra practicality. Even by 1970s standards, this was a basic machine. *(Suzuki GB)*

always?). They described the LJ series as being a range of '…ultimately rationalized cars' and referred to the interior as '…an excellent example of functionality without the nonsense frills'.

There wasn't even an enormous amount of choice when it came to picking a colour for your 1979-model LJ80. You could have whatever you wanted, as long as it was light blue, red or white. No metallics, no blacks – but what did this matter to most buyers? A workhorse doesn't have to be pretty to be good at its job.

The cheapest LJ in the line-up was sold simply as the LJ80, politely known as an open-top vehicle, but more accurately described as a no-top vehicle. That's right … you could actually buy a brand spanking new LJ80 with absolutely nothing in the way of weather equipment, or even doors. If you really wanted to experience the

and appeal. If you wanted luxury, you looked elsewhere and spent a lot more; if you wanted honest, no-nonsense transport, you turned to Suzuki.

The copywriters for the LJ's first British brochure of 1978 managed to turn the model's lack of creature comforts into something of a positive (don't they

Above: You didn't get a lot in the way of equipment or instrumentation inside your Suzuki LJ – but that didn't bother most buyers of this honest workhorse. Even the radio and cigarette lighter fitted here were both optional extras when new. UK-spec models obviously came with right-hand drive. *(Suzuki GB)*

Right: In photographs, the LJ80's timeless, Jeep-like styling gives the model an almost masculine appearance. That's why, when you see one 'in the metal' for the first time, its diminutive size and stature can come as something of a shock. *(Suzuki GB)*

ravages of the weather, you could fold the windscreen flat and enjoy the sensation of streaming eyes to go with your rain-soaked head and torso. In reality though, most examples of the LJ80 came with both a fabric roof and tubular-framed fabric doors, with black as 'standard' or white available as an 'optional extra'. Suzuki really knew how to spoil those rag-top fans of the 1970s!

Rather more 'sensible' than the LJ80 (in the UK, at least) was the LJ80V – a three-door hard-top version which actually offered decent weather protection. It provided a glimpse into the future too, for this was the version of the LJ that is perhaps most recognisable as the predecessor of the later SJ, Samurai and even Jimny

Above: You are now entering a hard-hat area! A sensible precaution when driving a roofless LJ cross-country, despite the optional roll bar fitted to this example. *(Suzuki GB)*

Right: The LJ's 797cc overhead-cam engine was an advanced design by the standards of the '70s, and its maximum output of 41bhp was perfectly respectable for such a tiny capacity. Thanks to the vehicle's lightweight design, LJ80 performance could almost be described as 'lively'. *(Suzuki GB)*

WHAT SUZUKI SAID: The LJ80V (Hard-top)

'The LJ80V is a van type vehicle that has the dual ability to appeal to those persons needing closed body construction comfort, yet sturdy and powerful performance of four-wheel drive functionality. The light kerb weight of 785kg in combination with the powerful engine assures top-notch running performance.'

models. Using straight lines, a boxy rear, a large side-hinged tailgate, a rear-mounted spare wheel and an abundance of common sense in its appearance, the LJ80V set a style that future small Suzuki 4x4s would follow.

Interestingly, the 'V' in LJ80V reputedly stood for 'van', despite this being a fully windowed 4x4 which, in most instances, was supplied as a four-seater. Remove the back seats though (assuming they were fitted in the first place) and this would indeed make a hugely useful, go-anywhere holdall.

The third version of the LJ80 available from 1978 was the awkwardly named LJ81K, a hard-top two-door pick-up that was quite unlike anything else on the market back then. Admittedly, Land Rover did have a short-wheelbase pick-up derivative of their Series III model – but, as with the rest of their range, this was dramatically more expensive than Suzuki's offering. Despite a maximum carrying weight of just 250kg (a quarter of a tonne isn't much by pick-up standards), the LJ81K proved to be a useful workhorse.

Whether it was hauling around bales of straw or the odd stray sheep, the LJ81K was an invaluable light truck, as Suzuki themselves were quick to point out: 'It's excellent for doing whatever you heretofore thought out-of-the-question', they reckoned. An awkward-sounding description, but an accurate one. What a shame then, that this is an area of the market which, in later years, Suzuki has totally deserted in Europe, despite the current popularity of four-wheel-drive pick-up trucks. Can you imagine how useful a little Jimny pick-up would be? Sadly, it has never happened.

The LJ80 now

I have already explained that the Suzuki LJ80 is now a rare vehicle in the UK. Indeed, it is, or, at least, it is in standard form. A reasonable number of upgraded, uprated and seriously modified examples survive amongst the off-road fraternity, employed solely for off-road fun days and competition use. They often bear little visual (or mechanical) resemblance to their original specification, having been given a new lease of life by their enthusiastic owners, but at least they live on in one form or another.

As for road-going, completely standard LJ80s … well, that is a different issue altogether. Any 4x4 workhorse will be rare to find in immaculate, cherished condition as it gets older, and the Suzuki LJ80 is no exception. If you come across one now, it is worth snapping up, although even the finest examples aren't worth a fortune these days, as we shall see in a later chapter.

In the UK though, there is an LJ80 that is almost certainly the sole exception to the rule. The last time I heard about it, this amazing example from 1982 was owned – but not used – by an avid Suzuki enthusiast. Incredibly, even by 2003, it had covered a mere 300-odd miles from new. The vehicle (PJX 490X) was later advertised on the eBay auction website and, it seems, changed hands within a couple of weeks.

Although the LJ80 series wasn't the biggest-selling 4x4 of its time, let's not underestimate its importance throughout Europe. If nothing else, it introduced potential buyers to the idea of an off-road Suzuki, and for the SJ series that was to follow in 1982, that was a crucial head-start.

4x4s didn't come any more utilitarian than the open-top LJ80. Fold the screen flat and you had the ultimate 'wind in the hair' experience! *(Suzuki GB)*

Chapter **Two**

SJ, Santana and Samurai

If 1978 had been a massively important year for Suzuki, marking the introduction of their LJ 4x4 models to European markets, then 1982 ran it a close second. This was the year when the vital new SJ, the eventual successor to the LJ, took a bow. It was also the year when all-wheel-drive Suzukis started appealing to a greater range of potential buyers than ever before.

Despite being based on the same separate-chassis principles as the LJ, the new SJ410 was a more 'grown-up' contender in the 4x4 market. This was not in terms of size, for the SJ series was almost as diminutive in dimensions and stature as its predecessor. However, it was a slightly more sophisticated and vastly more driveable vehicle. This was at a time when Britain's

small-car market was dominated by the likes of the Austin Mini Metro and MkI Ford Fiesta so it is no wonder an important minority of new-car buyers were looking for something a little more characterful and fun to drive.

This was an important shift, both in terms of Suzuki's thinking and the needs of a whole new breed of buyers. The LJ, which had first introduced Europeans to the idea of a tiny 4x4 from Suzuki, was very much a working tool. It had a job to do, and in the main it appealed to

The fresh-looking SJ series was a more sophisticated, better-equipped vehicle than the LJ it replaced in 1982. Its styling was still square and boxy, but far more in tune with 1980s tastes. *(Suzuki GB)*

With a few concessions to cosmetics – including metallic paint and side graphics – the SJ series was the first Suzuki 4x4 to see itself marketed as a 'lifestyle' vehicle. Before too long, it was being promoted as a genuine alternative to more conventional cars. *(Suzuki GB)*

commercial buyers who admired its go-anywhere capabilities and its value for money, but who didn't expect anything in the way of creature comforts. It wasn't the kind of vehicle that somebody who had previously owned a Renault 5 say, would seriously consider buying.

The SJ410 was different however, and yes, it was just as useful a workhorse as the LJ80 had ever been. It was also quicker, handled marginally better, was more sophisticated, was more comfortable and was generally more practical in day-to-day use. It meant that, for the first time ever, buyers of cheap and cheerless 'super-minis' had a genuine and interesting all-wheel-drive alternative waiting for them at their nearest Suzuki dealership.

It must be stressed though, that the use of such words as 'sophisticated' and 'comfortable' should all be taken in context. I'm comparing the SJ410 with the incredibly utilitarian LJ80, a vehicle that made a skateboard look luxurious. Comparing the SJ410 with the small hatch-backs which, price-wise, it found itself up against, you would discover that almost all of them were smoother to drive, more cosseting to ride in and arguably easier to live with. Yet for a small but growing number of new-car buyers, such considerations didn't seem to matter all that much.

The SJ series ended up being a serious hit in the UK. Sales built steadily from late 1982 onwards, and even the arrival of the far more developed and all-new Vitara in 1988 failed to damage them too much initially. Indeed, by the time the very last of the SJ series models, by then known simply as the Samurai, had been sold in the UK in 1997, a total of 34,500 examples had found buyers. This meant an average of 2,300 sales a year (although annual figures for the 1980s were actually far in excess of that). This was a figure which made the earlier LJ80's average annual sale of just 475 UK-spec cars look very poor in comparison.

Start of the SJ

That the Suzuki SJ was developed so much during its life says a lot about the competence of its original, basic design. Indeed, the fact that the SJ – in Samurai guise – lives on and is still produced in Spain at the time of writing is an amazing feat for what is now an aged design. Suzuki's designers obviously got something very right indeed way back in 1982.

Like the LJ80 before, the SJ410 did not initially pretend to be anything other than a cheap and cheerful off-road machine. But as soon as anybody more used to an LJ80 experienced an SJ410 for the first time, they knew this was a far more accomplished design, even if it did lack some of the LJ's cheeky character.

Under the bonnet of the SJ410 sat a 970cc version of Suzuki's much-praised OHC four-cylinder unit. Admit-tedly, it only pushed out a mere 45bhp at 5,500rpm, an increase of just 4bhp over the LJ80 before, but with a relatively healthy torque figure of 54lb ft at 3,000rpm, this always felt like an eager and willing little car in most conditions. Push it towards the 70mph limit on the nearest motorway and the SJ410 would start to feel breathless; but used as a nimble and lively little run-about, it was more than capable of keeping up with other traffic.

The SJ410's power was transmitted via a basic four-speed gearbox to begin with, although a five-speed unit did arrive on the scene later on. This helped greatly on lengthy journeys, reducing revs and improving the SJ's long-distance fuel consumption.

As with the LJ80, the SJ410 offered part-time four-wheel drive, selectable via a two-speed transfer box. Standard road use saw rear-wheel drive employed, while off-road situations meant a choice of either high- or low-ratio gearing depending on the severity of the terrain. Just like the LJ, the SJ410 proved itself to be a formidable off-roader, its combination of all-wheel-drive traction, decent ground clearance, ultra-short wheelbase and useful lack of weight all coming together to create a rough-stuff vehicle of surprising capabilities.

WHAT SUZUKI SAID: The SJ Series

'Much of Suzuki's marketing effort has been directed at the creation of an outstandingly strong and individual image for the SJ and there is little doubt that it has become established, in a very short space of time, as a 'cult' car with a devoted – almost fanatical – following from its enthusiastic owners who regard it with the same affection as those who cherished their Beetles and Minis in the Sixties.'

New, 970cc and 1,324cc engines meant the SJ range offered improved performance and a less tiring experience than the good old LJ80 workhorse that had gone before. Even so, the basic SJ410 could never be seen as an ideal long-distance machine. *(Author)*

The suspension set-up on the new SJ410 was pretty standard, with front and rear live axles supported by leaf springs and telescopic dampers. Likewise, the low-tech recirculating ball-and-nut steering was as basic as was possible, despite providing the little Suzuki with, for the time, an impressively sharp feel.

The braking system though, was a major improvement over the LJ80's, thanks to the use of self-adjusting rear drums combined with front disc brakes. Not all early SJs came with servo-assisted brakes, which sometimes meant a fairly heavy stamp from your right foot in order to bring them to a rapid halt. That aside, the SJ410's braking capabilities were impressive for the time.

On board the SJ410, things were drastically improved too. Even the most basic versions came with what

Above: With a 'proper' dashboard and a few more mod cons on board, the Suzuki SJ had a broader appeal than its predecessor. This wasn't just a working vehicle; it was also perfectly useable as a second car or an urban runabout. *(Suzuki GB)*

Below: A wider range of colours was gradually introduced as the SJ series developed, although Peruchet Red and plain old white remained two of the most popular. *(Suzuki GB)*

looked like a 'proper' dashboard and the use of plastics instead of bare, painted metal. Seats were also improved, although even the most avid Suzuki enthusiast would admit that on a long haul they weren't as supportive as they could have been. But what did that really matter? The SJ410 was a rugged and durable little beast, just like its LJ80 predecessor, and that is what people wanted from their small Suzuki 4x4 … wasn't it?

SJ410 – the evolution begins

The SJ range was fairly restricted to begin with. This probably came as no surprise, given the fact that the LJ before it had only ever been available in a maximum of three different versions, but, unlike its predecessor, the SJ was destined for far greater development later on in its life.

To begin with, we were offered what the importers called simply the SJ410 Passenger Car and SJ410 Van, although the latter was to become known as the awkwardly named SJ410VB JA in later years. Both models did exactly what they claimed to do, offering impressive go-anywhere abilities in a small, cheap and

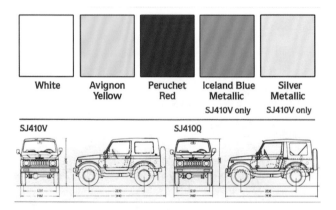

| White | Avignon Yellow | Peruchet Red | Iceland Blue Metallic | Silver Metallic |
| | | | SJ410V only | SJ410V only |

WHAT SUZUKI SAID: The SJ410

'Suzuki is the world's largest manufacturer of purpose-built, lightweight four-wheel drive vehicles, and all of Suzuki's 30 years of experience in engine and chassis technology have gone into the development of the SJ410 range. Rugged four-wheel drive practicality gives the SJ410 a true, go-anywhere ability that simply isn't matched by other so-called off-road vehicles.'

Above: The author bought this used and abused, but fully MoT'd SJ410 back in 2002 for just £400 – proof that an elderly SJ really can offer great value for money. He became its 17th proud owner... *(Author)*

Left: The non-original soft-top on this example looks horrid, but at least it's waterproof. That still doesn't prevent dreadful condensation problems inside the vehicle though! *(Author)*

likeable package. They were visually similar, with the van obviously lacking the rear side windows and back seat of the 'car' version. Each appealed to what had quickly become a loyal band of Suzuki converts, with commercial users and private buyers alike being impressed with the SJ410's spec and capabilities.

It wasn't long though, before arguably the most important SJ derivative arrived on the UK scene: the SJ410 soft-top. Like the rag-top LJ80 that had gone before, the newcomer appealed to open-air fans who

wanted the thrills of a convertible combined with the capabilities of an off-roader. Unlike the LJ though, the open-air SJ came with such 'luxuries' as proper steel doors instead of the previous model's flimsy canvas affairs.

No wonder then, that the SJ Soft-top was seen as more of a recreational fun car than a commercial workhorse. Here was a cheap and cheerful machine that, when the mood took you and the sun was shining, could soon be transformed into an open-top cruiser, ideal for posing along Brighton seafront or for turning heads amongst the surfers of Newquay. But during the other 300 odd days of the year (when the weather was not so good), its good-quality canvas hood, steel doors and impressive heater would ensure its occupants were snug and comfortable, well, sort of.

The downside was that the SJ's fabric roof took a long time to refit in its original position, thanks to an abundance of press-studs and zips. Once in place, it never seemed to look quite as it did when it first rolled off the Suzuki assembly line. Many an owner got wet while desperately trying to refit their Suzuki's hood when the sun disappeared behind a huge rain cloud. This was indeed the ideal vehicle for cruising around southern Spain in … but for Britain, well that was perhaps a different story.

Suzuki needn't have worried though, for whatever its downfalls might have been, the SJ Soft-top soon established itself as the best-seller of the early SJ410 range. For the first time ever, here was an all-wheel-drive Suzuki that was being bought for its head-turning charms rather than its workmanlike efficiency. And that was an important turning point, not only for this successful Japanese manufacturer but for the 4x4 market in general.

In everyday use, the extra power of the SJ413 came in useful. It was faster, more refined and tended not to run out of steam so easily on long motorway hauls. (Suzuki GB)

SJ413 – more power, more refinement

Appealing to a new breed of consumer and almost creating a new class of vehicle is all well and good, but it puts added pressure on any manufacturer to continue the development of its model range before the competition catches up – or even beats you at your own game.

For three years, the SJ410 continued to establish itself in Europe and the UK's steadily expanding 4x4 market, the little Suzuki having this bottom end of the market more or less to itself. There was still no other company selling quite such a tiny or inexpensive 4x4 as the SJ410 in the early 1980s, and that meant a loyal following, a steady stream of customers, and a need for further development.

By 1985, just seven years after Suzuki first took the brave step of launching into Britain's up-and-coming 4x4 scene, this most successful of Japan's 'specialist' makers realised there was a need for a new SJ. There was little wrong with the original basic design, of course, but as the company's customer base was steadily changing from 'commercial' to 'lifestyle', potential buyers were asking for more

power, more refinement and a generally upgraded driving experience.

That is exactly what they got in 1985, with the arrival of the SJ413. Propelled by an all-alloy 1,324cc four-cylinder powerplant, the SJ413 offered a useful 63bhp (up 18bhp on the SJ410) at 6,000rpm, with 73.7lb ft of torque also in its favour. Most examples came with five-speed transmission too, which obviously helped to make motorway cruising and non-urban journeys vastly more pleasurable.

All else about the SJ413 was pretty much as for the '410, except when it came to standard equipment. Suzuki's top-of-the-range SJ413VJX model came with such luxuries as reclining, cloth-covered front seats, integral head restraints, a tachometer and a few other 'niceties'. The SJ range was growing up fast – and the more powerful, better-equipped SJ413 was proof of that.

Santana saunters in

We touched earlier on the SJ model's increased appeal as a 'lifestyle' vehicle, a far cry from the commercial-based interest of the earlier LJ80. This unique new customer base first started to build with the introduction of the SJ410 Soft-top back in 1983, but it was in early 1987 that the whole process really started to gain momentum, for that was when the long-awaited Santana derivative finally arrived in the UK.

The Santana was a hugely important vehicle for Suzuki GB Cars (the importers of the time) in two ways. First, it was Suzuki's first official 'lifestyle' version of the SJ series to hit the streets, with unashamed concessions to cosmetics and frivolities in an effort to appeal to a new breed of buyer, while secondly, it was the first Suzuki 4x4 imported into the UK that was not built in Japan – shock, horror!

In fact, the Suzuki Santana was the result of a joint venture between the Suzuki Motor Company and the Land Rover Santana factory at Linares in Spain. By 1987, when the Santana version of the SJ arrived in Britain, Suzuki owned a 20 per cent stake in the Spanish

If you thought all Suzuki Santanas were powered by 1.3-litre engines, you're probably confusing them with the later Samurai. Early Santanas came only with the SJ410's 970cc four-pot unit. *(Suzuki GB)*

firm – an involvement that was set to grow over the coming years. So there was the bizarre situation where Spanish-spec Land Rovers were rolling out of the same factory as Spanish-built Suzukis – an unprecedented situation by 1980s standards.

The plan was a clever one. After all, this was one of the neatest ways that Suzuki could avoid the restrictive import quotas that existed on Japanese-built cars in the 1980s. By building the Santana exclusively in Spain, Suzuki could bring as many of them in to Britain as it could realistically sell. This freed up the rest of their Japanese-car quota to boost imports of their other models, including the relatively new front-wheel drive Swift 'supermini'.

Interestingly, Suzuki did not make too much of a feature of the Santana's Spanish origins when the new model took a bow. In a Santana brochure from May 1987, the copywriters simply said: 'The new Suzuki Santana is built entirely at a factory which specialises in the manufacture of four-wheel-drive vehicles – maintaining our reputation for quality and reliability.' They forgot to mention that the factory was in Spain, a country less renowned for the build quality and reliability of its cars than Japan was back in 1987.

The Santana was quite a hit and two versions were available initially, with what Suzuki described in a February 1987 press release as: '… exclusively designed body stripes and interiors for the British market'. These comprised the simply named Santana (finished all in white) and the more exciting sounding Santana Sport (which, by contrast, was all black). Mechanically though, they were identical, sharing the same 970cc OHC engine but now linked to a five-speed transmission as standard.

In a press release of the time, Suzuki GB Cars was keen to stress the Santana's move away from the commercial market towards the private buyer who was looking for inexpensive, wind-in-the-hair fun. When it came to standard equipment, they were soon boasting about the Santana's '… special colour co-ordinated deluxe cloth interior, split rear seats, servo-assisted brakes and softer suspension for improved on-road ride'. No pre-1987 Suzuki SJ derivative had ever been as well equipped or as pleasant to drive as the Santana.

The arrival of the Santana also saw the introduction of more Suzuki accessories and options than ever

before – something this new breed of buyer was now demanding. The kind of folk who bought brand-new Santanas were also the type of people who wanted to make their vehicles stand out even more from the crowd. No wonder then, that Suzuki was soon doing a good trade in bull bars, roll bars, surf board bars and even inclinometers, although just how many Santana buyers embarked upon the kind of serious off-roading that made the latter item invaluable, is not known.

The newcomer's list price of £6,499 made it an affordable and fun-loving alternative to Europe's more conventional small cars of the time. It comes as no surprise that poseurs and attention-seekers took to the Santana in a big way. It wasn't long before this latest model from Suzuki was being spotted parked outside hairdressers' salons throughout the UK. It is amazing just what Suzuki managed to achieve with a bit of colour-coding, some stripes and a modicum of extra equipment…

The commercials

Despite the SJ series' move towards the new-found 'lifestyle' scene, Suzuki was keen not to lose its grip on the lightweight 4x4 commercial market either. Right from the start, the SJ410 was available as a panel van, as mentioned earlier. It took a little longer for the SJ413K to arrive though, as a longer-wheelbase, two-seater pick-up truck, essentially a direct replacement for the old LJ81K.

Powered by the same 1,324cc engine as the SJ413VJX, this truck combined the neat front-end styling of the standard SJ with a usefully sized (1,550 x 1,320mm) pick-up bed bringing up the rear. The dropsides and tailgate made the pick-up easy to load with even fairly heavy items, which was fortunate really, as the newcomer was able to lug around loads of up to 455kg in weight, a massive improvement over the old LJ81K's maximum payload of just 250kg.

As a towing vehicle too, this 1.3-litre light truck was a useful tool, with a maximum towing capacity of 1,100kg in the case of a braked trailer. This was extremely useful for the farmers and agriculturalists at whom the truck was aimed. Suddenly, they didn't have to invest in an expensive new Land Rover in order to haul trailers and equipment over rough terrain.

Despite its obvious advantages though, the SJ413K was not a major success for Suzuki GB Cars and it proved to be one of the shortest-surviving models in the UK line-up. Indeed, by the time 1987 dawned, the SJ commercial range consisted solely of the SJ410 Van and

Above: Suzuki was quick to make sure it didn't lose out on the pick-up market with the SJ, hence the introduction of the SJ413K derivative. Its maximum payload of 455kg was vastly more useful than the previous LJ81K's miserly 250kg capacity. Even so, sales weren't huge, despite the 413K's undoubted usefulness. *(Suzuki GB)*

Right: Back in 1987, Suzuki produced a separate brochure dedicated to the SJ commercials. By then though, the SJ413K 'proper' pick-up had been dropped from the UK range, leaving just the clumsily titled SJ410VB JA Van and SJ410QB JA Soft Top truck. *(Suzuki GB)*

the new Soft-top which was a two-seater, stripped-out 'truck' version of the open-top passenger-carrying model. Both featured easy-to-clean vinyl upholstery, rubber matting on the floor and a distinct lack of creature comforts. But as VAT-saving go-anywhere vehicles for commercial users on a tight budget, they were a tempting proposition.

Interestingly though, a version of the SJ413K – known as the Samurai Pick-up – is still produced in Spain, and does fairly well both in its home market and in Portugal. It has a dubiously restyled front end these days, giving it a bit of an awkward appearance, but it is good to know it still lives on.

The Samurai Pick-up isn't the only version of the 'bigger' SJ design to remain in production though. People often forget that even in the UK we were treated to a long-wheelbase passenger-carrying version of the SJ, still offering just four seats but with extra luggage space available. This model also still survives, albeit in India where it is built and sold as the Maruti Gypsy King (strange, but true). That particular bodyshell may not

have been a big hit in the fashion-conscious UK market, but in India it is still seen as a worthy and useful all-wheel-drive workhorse.

And on to the Samurai . . .

By the end of the 1980s, the SJ and Santana series was a relatively aged design. Things moved fast in the motoring world even back then, and a model that had been around since 1982 was already being viewed as fairly old before the decade was out.

Obviously, the big news for Suzuki during the late 1980s was the introduction of the vital new Vitara, which will be covered in the next chapter. But in its own way, the launch of the Suzuki Samurai was also a major event. Introduced to the UK in 1989, the new-spec Samurai took the original SJ concept another step forward, ensuring this 'old soldier' had plenty more to offer buyers in the 1990s.

The engine was initially the same 1,324cc unit that had given such good service in the SJ413 previously. All Samurais came with five-speed transmission

Commercials

Above: The SJ410VB JA hard-top van was a useful little tool, offering a generously roomy load area capable of carrying up to 270kg. It was a hard-working machine and, with a towing capacity of up to 1,100kg, was extremely versatile too. *(Suzuki GB)*

Right: By the time the 1995 model year arrived and the Samurai was nearing the end of its time on sale in the UK, it had matured into a relatively luxurious and comfortable 4x4 compared with those rather more basic early SJs. *(Suzuki GB)*

as standard, linked to the simple dual-range transfer box that had proved so effective over the years.

Before too long though, the Samurai found itself with a new engine under its bonnet – still of 1.3-litre capacity (or 1,298cc, to be exact), but this time pumping out a more competitive 68bhp at 6,000rpm. Torque levels increased slightly too, with 76lb ft on tap at a usefully low (by petrol engine standards) 3,500rpm. This new engine also saw the fitment of single-point fuel-injection in place of the previous carburettor set-up, as well as the soon-to-be-obligatory catalytic converter.

Interestingly, Suzuki eventually introduced a 1.9-litre turbo-diesel version of the Samurai, although strangely not for UK consumption. This proved a popular, lively and incredibly economical choice for 4x4 buyers in mainland Europe. Surely then, the decision not to sell it in the UK is one of the ultimate examples of a wasted opportunity?

As with the Santana before it, the Samurai found itself with softened suspension settings in an attempt

to cure the SJ of its bone-jarring ride. To a certain extent it was successful in this, although its ride quality could never be described as 'supple', even by its biggest fans.

Fans and followers were never in short supply with the Spanish-built Samurai. By the time the 1990s dawned, and despite its basic design being eight years old by then, the Samurai was achieving almost cult status in the UK and throughout mainland Europe. With special graphics, extra trimmings and – in many cases – alloy wheels as part of the package, any Samurai was an eye-catching and attractive fun car.

It was also better equipped inside than any other SJ before. By the time the Samurai was in its twilight years, it was offering (for the 1995 model year) bucket-shaped front seats with head restraints, a lockable glovebox, a digital clock, individually folding rear seats and a grab rail. Externally, it featured what Suzuki optimistically referred to as a 'deluxe hood', as well as flared wheel-arches for a more stylish look.

By the mid-1990s, just one version of the Samurai remained on sale in the UK: the 1.3-litre Soft-top. Both the hard-top version of 1989 and the little-known long-wheelbase derivative of the following year had both long since disappeared. The open-air Samurai was the sole survivor of a range of compact 4x4s that had proved so popular in Britain.

With more versions of the hugely successful Vitara being launched throughout the 1990s, the Samurai found itself becoming increasingly redundant in the modern world. People were willing to spend a little extra to get what most considered a superior vehicle, in the shape of the trendy Vitara. The Samurai, as far as the British market was concerned, was finally consigned to the history books.

The safety issue

We couldn't write a chapter on the Suzuki SJ series without mentioning the safety concerns that first arose in 1988. These started in the UK, when the consumer magazine *Which?* criticised the SJ for what it considered to be its potentially dangerous handling. Britain's

Below: With the right kind of mud-plugging tyres fitted, any old SJ will make a great off-road fun car. Shown here are a couple of 410s taking part in an organised fun day, one of the most inexpensive ways of enjoying some non-competitive off-roading.

(John Richardson)

The driver of this **SJ Soft Top** shows just what can be achieved with some off-road rubber, a home-made snorkel and a roll cage. This little Suzuki showed many a larger machine just how it should be done at an off-road event in 2004. *(Author)*

Consumers' Association was soon accusing the SJ of being unstable and unsafe.

This created more than a few negative headlines about the SJ series, particularly amongst the British tabloid press. Word spread to the USA too, where consumers' organisations were similarly critical. It was a potential PR disaster for Suzuki in general and the SJ in particular.

Happily, some of the British motoring press were able to be more supportive of the various SJ models,

This 2002-model Spanish-spec Samurai was still giving reliable service as a hire car in Gran Canaria at the time of writing. Battered and unloved, it was a brilliant performer – particularly over the rocky, mountainous terrain of the Canary Islands. *(Author)*

and were more realistic in their outlook. Obviously, no magazine could ever claim that it was impossible to 'roll' an SJ. After all, any tall, narrow, short-wheelbase vehicle when pushed into an unsuitable manoeuvre will have more of a tendency to roll over than a conventional car might. But most commentators seemed to accept that for an SJ to topple, it would have to be driven in a reckless style that was completely alien to most owners.

What could have been a disastrous situation for the

Boot space was never a plus point for the short-wheelbase Vitara, although at least the split/fold back seat – standard from the earliest models – aided versatility. Used as a two-seater, even the smallest Vitaras made decent load-carriers.
(Frank Westworth)

Still, at least the little Vitara 1.6 JLX came as standard with a five-speed gearbox, helping to make this the most capable motorway-driving Suzuki 4x4 yet seen. It could cruise at the legal speed limit all day, without any of the strain or instability that drivers of SJs could sometimes be heard to complain about.

Much of the Vitara's impressive stability came from its bigger dimensions. The newcomer was 7in longer and 6in wider than the original SJ, which gave the Vitara a more impressive stance and the promise of 'flatter' cornering – despite the fact that it was also somewhat taller than an SJ.

It wasn't just the Vitara's dimensions which gave this new model an improved driving experience and decent handling though; there was also a more sophisticated suspension system slung underneath. The Vitara's independent set-up comprised coil springs and MacPherson struts – a straightforward, well-proven and extremely effective arrangement.

Like all previous 4x4 Suzukis, the Vitara came with a

WHAT THE PRESS SAID:

'A brilliant piece of marketing by Suzuki, picking up sales from would-be owners of larger, more expensive "image" off-roaders. All the creature comforts of a hatchback, with power steering and electric windows available as extras, in a good-looking three-door body.' (Martin Lewis, A-Z of Cars of the 1980s)

dual-range transfer box, with rear-wheel drive reserved for road use and a choice of two ratios of all-wheel drive for when the going got tough. Braking was by discs up front with drums bringing up the rear, although at this stage the idea of a Vitara with ABS hadn't been thought of – not even as an extra-cost option.

Equipment levels weren't high by the standards of other £9,000 cars. There was no power steering, no electric windows, sunroof or sound system of any kind, but you did get electrically adjustable door mirrors, a split/fold rear seat and a height-adjustable steering wheel thrown in for your money.

Compared like-for-like with the 'hot hatches' that the new Vitara found itself up against, this latest Suzuki seemed slow and under-equipped. The extra variations and different derivatives that were waiting in the wings however would ensure this vital newcomer's appeal would soon be spreading.

The range expands

Never a company slow to exploit a situation, Suzuki made sure the Vitara range was quick to expand. If this vital new vehicle was to enjoy the kind of widespread appeal its makers were hoping for, a diversity of different models was essential, as soon as possible.

By the time the range started to grow, the Vitara was faced with an impressive new rival: the long-awaited Daihatsu Sportrak. Of similar size to the Vitara, the Sportrak was also a two-door 'lifestyle' 4x4 powered by a 1.6-litre engine, and while it may not have been as outwardly trendy-looking as its Suzuki rival, you couldn't knock it as a package. By 1991 (with three versions of the Daihatsu on sale by then), the Sportrak 1.6 STi was a tempting buy at £10,515. Happily for Suzuki though, the least-expensive Vitara 1.6 JLX was usefully cheaper at £9,899 in the UK at that time.

While Suzuki still had value for money on their side, they had to watch out when it came to dynamics. The 1991 Sportrak, for example, came with the promise of

The long-wheelbase five-door Vitara may have lacked the smaller version's 'funkiness', but it was a more practical machine in almost every respect. At last, there was a Vitara for the family car buyer. Shown here is a 1993 entry-level JX version, complete with black bumpers. *(Suzuki GB)*

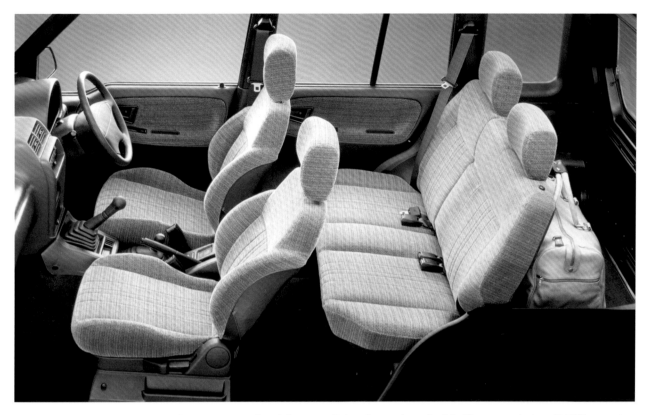

Above: Not only was there more space for passengers on board the five-door Vitara, it even had a decent amount of room for their luggage. Entry and exit to and from the back seat was obviously a lot easier than with the three-door versions! *(Suzuki GB)*

Below: At opposite ends of the Vitara range in the mid-1990s were the fun-loving Soft Top and the rather more staid five-door Estate. Each appealed to different buyers, for obvious reasons – proving that a single model range really can traverse several vehicle classes. *(Suzuki GB)*

Above: It wasn't long before Vitara owners realised just how 'personalised' they could make their vehicles. At one time, no two Vitaras seemed to be the same, such was their popularity with boy racers and the McDonald's crowd! *(Author)*

Below: It's Britain, it's raining and this Vitara's hood is firmly in the upright position. No wonder the soft-top model proved such a major hit in the sunnier climes of southern Europe. *(Frank Westworth)*

excellent performance by 4x4 standards – with a top speed of 93mph and a power output of 95bhp. By comparison, the Vitara JLX of the time offered just 80bhp, despite the recent adoption of fuel-injection.

The solution to any advantages the Daihatsu Sportrak might have had was for Suzuki to get cracking with launching new versions of the Vitara. By the time both models were proving their worth and selling well at the start of the 1990s, the all-important Vitara was available in three-door hard-top, two-door soft-top and five-door long-wheelbase estate guises.

At that stage, all versions of the Vitara were still powered by Suzuki's 1,590cc four-pot. Amazingly, you could still buy an ultra-basic version of the 1.6 JLX with a single carburettor, although most derivatives had gone over to fuel-injection by then. All fuel-injected Vitaras came with catalytic converters, in readiness for legislation the following year dictating all new petrol-engined cars in the UK had to have 'cats' as standard.

The trendiest of the Vitaras throughout the model's life was the convertible – the beloved transport of hairdressers and attention seekers through the 1990s. Although this version certainly had its

shortcomings (including a roof that took far too long to fold or remove, and to reverse the process again when it started raining), it proved to be a massive hit.

It was particularly popular in southern Europe, where the favourable climate allowed the hood to be stowed away most of the time, and the Vitara's occupants could be topping up their tans while cruising around. On the streets of rainy Manchester or snowy Glasgow, the advantages of the rag-top Vitara were less obvious.

But this didn't seem to matter. Here was a vehicle which, more than any compact 4x4 that had gone before, was developing a cult following. It was affordable to buy, cheap to run, fantastic looking – and it answered the needs of so many buyers in the early '90s. Of course, it was a lot more 'grown-up' than any of the SJ derivatives of the '80s.

At the other end of the trendiness scale was the long-wheelbase Vitara mentioned earlier. Measuring 16in more than the short-wheelbase in overall length, this new estate was destined to be the most practical model in the line-up. While many (mainly younger) buyers were happy to put trendiness higher

Opposite: 'Added appeal for the 4x4 Trend Setter' was how Suzuki described some minor enhancements for the 1997 model year. Nine years on from its launch, the Vitara range was proving more popular than ever. *(Suzuki GB)*

Above: The most powerful Vitara finally arrived in the shape of the 135 bhp 2.0-litre 24-valve V6, available in long-wheelbase guise only. It took the Vitara name further upmarket than its original designers had probably ever intended – but it was a decision that worked well. *(Suzuki GB)*

The original-style Vitara interior was fairly drab and uninspiring. Equipment levels weren't too impressive either. What a shame the inside of what was outwardly a fantastic looking vehicle was such a letdown. *(Frank Westworth)*

up their list of priorities than practicality, there were other potential buyers who needed a family-sized car.

For the first time, the Vitara was able to span several different vehicle classes, with the long-wheelbase proving to be a viable alternative to the dull and boring medium-size estates of the time, as well as giving other 4x4s a run for their money. Back in 1991, a

WHAT THE PRESS SAID:

'For: Looks the part; refined for a baby 4WD. Against: Ride a bit choppy; drab interior. Sum-up: Sloane Rangers, here we come.' *(Car, April 1989)*

Vitara 1.6 JLX SE five-door would have set you back £12,950 – roughly the same price as a Ford Escort 1.6 Ghia Estate or a Vauxhall Astra 1.8 SXi Estate. Rather than being seen at the wheel of an Escort or an Astra, increasing numbers of buyers could see the advantages of going the 'alternative' route – much to Suzuki's delight.

Inside story

Even the biggest fans of the Suzuki Vitara would struggle to call its interior anything other than functional. Admittedly, back in 1988 it represented a major step forward from the original SJ's, thanks to its softer appearance, 'proper' dashboard and reasonable ergonomics. But compared with the mainstream cars the Vitara found itself up against, the Suzuki was basic and unimaginative inside.

The motoring press agreed, often criticising the Vitara throughout its long life for the design of its interior. *Car* magazine referred to the inside of the Vitara as simply 'drab', and perhaps they were right.

Colours tended to be dark; upholstery was unattrac-
tive; the whole thing looked staid, while for a car that
outwardly looked so 'funky' and different, it was a
great shame.

The major instruments were housed in a
small, boxy-looking binnacle, while heater controls
and ancillaries could be found in the centre console
which led the way down to the gearstick and
transfer-box lever. Ahead of the front seat passenger
was a pull-down glovebox lid, on top of which was
a usefully large storage area. And that was it. The
whole thing was safe, uninspiring and a bit of a
letdown.

Am I being too harsh? Perhaps, but when you
look at the way the interiors of later 'lifestyle' 4x4s
evolved over the years (the Toyota RAV4 being one
of the best examples), it is hard not to be annoyed
that Suzuki played things so safely inside. They had
been adventurous externally, bringing to the market
a fun and trendy looking little 4x4 that was quite
unlike anything else around in 1988. So why not use

**Things improved slightly in later years, when the Vitara's instrument
binnacle was restyled and given a 'softer' appearance, and the whole
dashboard became rather more contemporary looking. Even so, it was
hardly the last word in luxury.** *(Author)*

the same degree of imagination when it came to
designing the interior? It is still a mystery.

The Vitara's interior was improved later in its life,
with a slightly softer-looking dashboard style
introduced – but even then it still looked way too
conventional. Still, at least Suzuki realised they should
offer buyers a little more luxury in later years, with
power steering, tinted glass, proper carpets, an optional
sunroof, rear wash/wipe and lots more appearing on
various models during the Vitara's career.

More engines

With the expansion of the Vitara's range of different
body options, Suzuki knew they couldn't rely on the
original 1.6-litre engine for ever. It was still a useful
and competitive unit, that was for sure, and particularly

so since the adoption of fuel-injection and a 16-valve cylinder head, which saw power output in the five-door version boosted to 95bhp by 1991. However, a choice of other engines would need to become available if the Vitara was to retain its competitive edge.

In the end, a good line-up of powerplants was offered. By 1996, the eight-valve version of the Vitara's 1,590cc engine – which ended up pushing out 79bhp – had been dropped. In its place, all 1.6-litre Vitaras were now 16-valve, with the 95bhp endowing the short-wheelbase versions with livelier performances at last. Vitara 1.6 16v models were available in short- or long-wheelbase forms, while a well-equipped SE version was available for those seeking more luxury.

Elsewhere in the Vitara range, 2.0-litre power had appeared, and in fact, a choice of two such engines was available by 1996, comprising a 71bhp intercooled turbo-diesel and a 135bhp twin-cam V6 petrol. The timing of both couldn't have been better: the turbo-diesel arrived just in time to cash in on rapidly expanding sales of diesel-powered 4x4s throughout Europe, while the petrol managed to pre-empt the launch of other V6-powered compact 4x4s by three or four years.

Both 2.0-litre Vitaras were available in five-door long-wheelbase form only, which was surely another very sound decision. Back in '96, buyers hadn't cottoned on to the fact that a diesel-powered car can still be fun, which meant that few enthusiasts of the short-wheelbase Vitaras would ever have considered buying a

The original Vitara's 1,590cc eight-valve engine was sufficient for 1988 – but Suzuki couldn't afford to become complacent. The engine was greatly improved later on, thanks to fuel-injection and a 16-valve cylinder head, boosting power from 75bhp to 90bhp. It helped to make the Vitara a much 'peppier' drive. *(Author)*

diesel version. And as for the V6 … well, can you imagine how 135bhp would feel under the bonnet of the smallest Vitara? At least the long-wheelbase design gave this 'performance' model a safer handling and roadholding experience.

The 21st century has seen fantastic progress in the development of diesel engines, with power outputs from the best examples now being on a par with their petrol-powered equivalents. No wonder then, that an output of 71bhp from the turbo-diesel Vitara seems very unimpressive today. Back in the 1990s though, it was a respectable figure by 4x4 standards, and what it lacked in speed compared with the petrol-engined Suzukis, it more than made up for in economy. Few owners would have seen fuel consumption fall much below 40mpg, which, for a family-size, five-door 4x4 of the time, was excellent.

Squeezing a V6 powerplant under the Vitara's bonnet was no mean feat – but Suzuki's 2.0-litre V6 was actually a remarkably compact engine. Note the raised central bonnet line and protruding front grille of the V6 Vitara. *(Suzuki GB)*

The owner of a Vitara V6, of course, could only dream of such economy. By any standards, the 135bhp Vitara was a thirsty beast, and you had to drive quite carefully to average even just 25mpg, but for some buyers, it was worth it. While the 2.0 V6 (one of the world's smallest production V6 engines, by the way) was the poorest-selling of all the Vitara powerplants over the years, it gave Suzuki a vital extra model to boast about taking the Vitara name further upmarket than ever before, into yet another sector.

A further major change that had occurred with the Vitara over the years was the introduction of automatic transmission as an optional extra. By the mid-1990s,

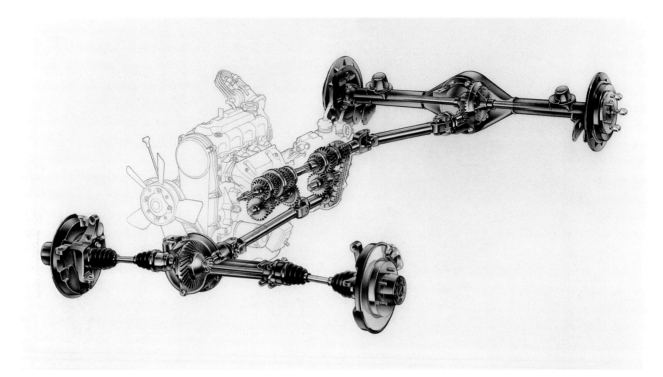

this was available on just about every version, which again helped to expand the Vitara line-up significantly. Automatic versions weren't massively popular, but they did help to ensure there was a Vitara to suit most tastes and by the time the transmission itself had matured into a four-speed set-up with lockable torque converter on third and fourth gears, it was quite a sophisticated arrangement.

The Vitara, in the space of just eight years, had gone from being a 'solo' model with niche appeal to a diverse and wide-ranging line-up. Despite the arrival of new, tougher competition as the 1990s wore on, the Vitara always maintained its competitive edge and, most importantly, its cult following.

Vitara off-road

As stated earlier, the Vitara was designed from scratch as a passenger-carrying road car first and foremost, but this doesn't mean Suzuki forgot to include some off-road capabilities in the final design; far from it. In fact, modified Vitaras are among the most competitive off-road Suzukis you're likely to see at all-terrain events throughout Europe, although in some cases, the modifications necessary to achieve this aren't so great.

Even as standard, the Vitara had the right ingredients: separate chassis for rigidity and torsional strength; dual-range transfer box; coil-sprung suspension; reasonable ground clearance; and – for the two- and

Suzuki's 4x4 know-how, gained through years of experience with the previous LJ and SJ models, came into its own when designing the Vitara. The part-time 4x4 set-up was simple and uncomplicated, but proved extremely effective. *(Suzuki GB)*

three-door models – a usefully short wheelbase with relatively little overhang at either end.

Select low-ratio four-wheel drive in any basic Vitara and you will find it is a perfectly adequate off-road machine for most people's needs. It is competent enough to get you out of trouble in reasonably rough terrain, and it's simple enough to provide lots of enjoyment and entertainment at any off-road fun day.

Perform the same antics in the same car but with a set of all-terrain tyres fitted and you'll see a massive difference. Lots more grip – as you'd expect – and what a simple and inexpensive transformation this is; so why didn't Suzuki equip the Vitara with different tyres from the start?

The simple answer is, because the customers wouldn't have liked them. Move away from road tyres and in the general direction of off-road rubber and you'll find the ride quality of your Vitara suffers alarmingly. Even a standard Vitara's ride can be 'choppy' at times, but with all-terrain tyres fitted, it is appalling. For any buyer of a brand-new Vitara back in the 1990s, that would have been unacceptable.

The nearest most new Vitaras ever came to going off-road was when they mounted the kerb on

Most of the very late UK-spec Vitaras tend to be examples of the 4u² model – which makes this basic 1999 example fairly scarce. It was put through its paces in 2003 by the author as part of a 'second-hand road test' for *4x4 Mart* magazine. *(Author)*

WHAT SUZUKI SAID: The Vitara 4u

'Whether a Soft-top with folding hood or an Estate with rear spoiler, both models have a commanding view of the road ahead and a unique style that only the Vitara can offer.'

Brighton seafront or trundled their way up a gravel driveway. So it was far more important for them to have the kind of rubber fitted that would give the best possible on-road ride, than it was for them to be able to traverse a muddy quarry or climb the side of a mountain.

The fact that most brand-new Vitaras rarely managed to display their genuine off-road capabilities was something of a waste. For anybody buying an elderly Vitara now however, with the sole intention of having some off-road fun, it is good news. It means that most examples won't have suffered previous off-road damage, and with the right kind of off-road tyres fitted

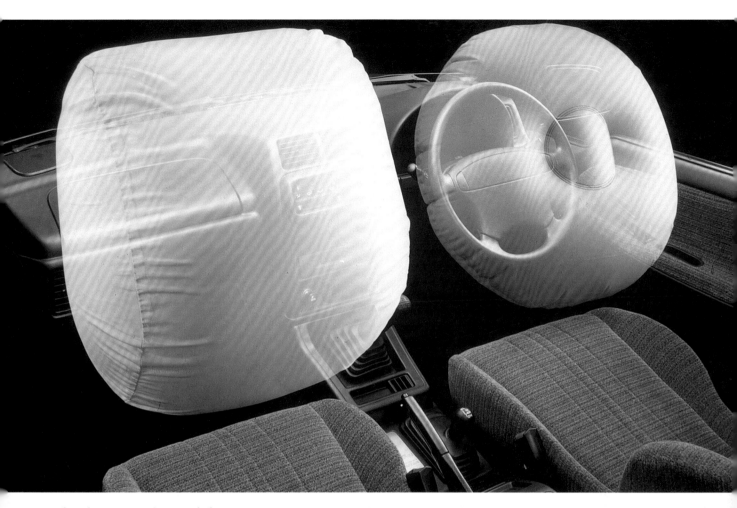

(and perhaps an engine snorkel to prevent water damage), you can go out there and have a great time without spending a fortune. Now is the time to release all those ex-hairdresser Vitaras back into the wild…

Over and out?

Even by Suzuki standards, the Vitara enjoyed a long and successful career throughout Europe. In the UK in particular, it gained itself the kind of loyal following that was perhaps rivalled only by Land Rover at the time. Vitara owners would defend their choice of vehicle with a vengeance, ignoring any suggestions that they didn't really need a 4x4, and enjoying instead the sheer usefulness, good looks and youthful appeal that the Vitara always offered.

All good things do come to an end however, and the eventual demise of the much-loved Vitara was an inevitability. Well, in the UK it was anyway. Thanks to the Santana Suzuki set-up, various versions of the Vitara are still being produced in Spain, mainly for local consumption. With a choice of 1.6 16-valve or HDI (diesel) power, in either three-door short-wheelbase or

Opposite: The 4u² model, announced in 1998, helped to breathe new life into the ageing but still much-loved Vitara. By this time, the long-wheelbase versions had been discontinued, effectively replaced by the new five-door Grand Vitara. *(Suzuki GB)*

Above: As the Vitara matured, so its previously sparse equipment levels improved. The range-topping 2.0-litre V6 five-door, for example, featured twin airbags as standard. Suzuki has never stopped trying to stay one step ahead of the competition. *(Suzuki GB)*

five-door long-wheelbase guises, there is still a Vitara being made to suit most Spanish tastes.

Head to southern Europe on holiday and you will see fleets of Spanish-built Vitaras for hire. While many of these are fairly long in the tooth, others are virtually brand new. I, for one, think it is fantastic that a compact 4x4 launched as long ago as 1988 can still find buyers and is still competitive all these years later.

In Britain though, the Vitara reached the end of the road in 2000. The Grand Vitara had been launched two years earlier, and as the newcomer's range had grown to incorporate the GV three-door models as well as the

One of the last UK-spec Vitaras – and proof that the original design hid its age incredibly well. Alloy wheels and graphics aside, this particular Vitara is virtually indistinguishable from a much earlier car. Rarely has there been a better example of stylists getting a vehicle's look 'just right' from 'day one'. *(Author)*

longer five-door versions, Suzuki GB decided there was no longer any need to import the original-type Vitara.

The final model to disappear from British price lists was the Vitara Commercial, a turbo-diesel-powered van derivative of the three-door model. Taking over from where the old SJ van had left off, this workhorse Vitara proved a capable and useful load-lugger for those whose budget wouldn't stretch any further. But even this model was gone by 2001.

Most popular of the late-model cars in the UK were the oddly named Vitara 4u and (subsequently) 4u^2, offered from 1998 in both three-door hard-top and two-door soft-top forms. With five-spoke alloy wheels, two-tone metallic paint, a rear spoiler (hard-top only) and other goodies as standard, the 4u and 4u^2 helped

breathe new life into what was by then a ten-year-old vehicle. Sales were respectable, and certainly helped to keep the Vitara alive in the UK for another couple of years.

With the popularity of the 4u and 4u^2, it is now quite unusual to see a basic, late-model Vitara on the road. This says a lot about the popularity of the various 'limited edition' Vitaras over the years, one of the most successful of which was the Vitara Verdi of 1994/95. Essentially, this was exactly the same vehicle as any other Vitara, but with different paint and a handful of extra gadgets. It was a ploy that worked well at the time, and with just 500 Vitara Verdis produced for the UK market, they sold out very quickly.

Many enthusiasts mourned the passing of the Vitara – and a lot of British fanatics still do. No wonder companies like Midlands-based Suzi Q's (mentioned again later) still do such a roaring trade in buying, selling and modifying Vitaras of all ages. The Vitara is the ultimate example of a Suzuki 4x4 that just refuses to lie down and die.

Vitaras are still a common sight these days on used car dealer forecourts throughout the country, with prices varying hugely according to age and exact specification. This superb 1999 soft-top was being sold in 2004 by Midlands-based Steve Smith Motor Company, and was featured at the time as part of a 'secondhand test' in *4x4 Mart* magazine. *(Author)*

Grand Vitara: Suzuki goes posh!

The arrival of the Vitara in 1988 had been crucial in helping Suzuki steer its way through what would be a rapidly changing 4x4 market in the '90s. Exactly ten years later, the company found itself in a similar position: the launch of the first of the Grand Vitaras in 1998 was a pivotal moment, as it gave an indication of exactly where Suzuki would be heading in the new Millennium.

Right from the start, the Grand Vitara five-door was marketed with family buyers very much in mind. It was arguably the most practical 4x4 that Suzuki had made to that time – although anybody used to buying their own petrol might have winced at the fuel consumption of the V6 version. *(Suzuki GB)*

'Further upmarket' was the general direction, many assumed – and bigger, too. In fact, the five-door Grand Vitara – the only body style available initially – was the largest Suzuki 4x4 to date, measuring 4,195mm in length and 1,780mm in width. It made even the long-wheelbase, five-door Vitara's dimensions look small at 4,013mm and 1,626mm respectively.

These might not sound like drastically varying measurements, but we shouldn't underestimate the importance of the difference. With their sights set firmly on their corporate crystal ball, Suzuki worked out that the 4x4 market of the early years of the 21st century was going to be maturing at incredible speed. Compact 4x4s, in particular, were destined to gain in popularity at

an unprecedented rate, which meant more new models from a wide range of different manufacturers would inevitably become available. If Suzuki was going to hold on to its reputation as the leading manufacturer of affordable, manageable, all-wheel-drive machines, it had to do something quite drastic.

And that is where the Grand Vitara came in. Interestingly, it was not the only all-new Suzuki 4x4 launched in 1998, for this was also the year when the cheap and cheerful Jimny hit the streets – but we'll come to that in the next chapter. Yes, in one single year,

WHAT SUZUKI SAID: The Grand Vitara

'This is a real 4x4 that is at home on the open road as it is coping with the rigours of the off-road track. The pedigree starts with a separate steel ladder-frame chassis that makes a sturdy but light base for the rest of the vehicle and provides protection against the roughest surfaces. Suzuki's innovative 'Drive Select 4x4' system allows you to change from 2WD to 4WD (high ratio) whilst on the move in a straight line … either off-road or on slippery surfaces, e.g. snow, ice, mud etc. When on tarmac and the vehicle is travelling in a straight line, you can simply change back to 2WD.'

Unlike some of its rivals – particularly Toyota's RAV4 – the new Grand Vitara could justifiably claim to be competent in most off-road situations. This certainly wasn't one of those 'all show and no go' 4x4s… (Suzuki GB)

Suzuki managed to neatly 'top-and-tail' its 4x4 range with the Grand Vitara and Jimny respectively, leaving the ten-year-old Vitara somewhere in the middle – both size-wise and price-wise.

New competition

Just as the Vitara was launched as a 'solo' model, with just one engine and one body style available initially, so the Grand Vitara followed suit. This time though, Suzuki decided to launch their newcomer from the top down, starting with the 2.5-litre V6 five-door, first shown to a European audience at the Geneva International Motor Show in March 1998.

In UK spec, the newcomer cost a not inconsiderable £16,370 when it went on sale – or £17,320 in four-speed automatic guise. By Suzuki standards, that was a heck of a lot of money and it was further upmarket than this manufacturer of affordable vehicles had ever gone before. Compared with the competition that was around that year however, it was positively good value.

It must be remembered, for example, that 1998 was also the year when the all-important Land Rover Freelander first hit the streets. This went on to become Europe's best-selling 4x4 fairly quickly; and in the UK, it shot from nowhere to market dominance almost overnight. Yet the Freelander did not have a hope of competing with the sheer value of the Grand Vitara.

The cheapest five-door Freelander Station Wagon back in '98 was the woefully basic 1.8i, a pricey piece of kit at £17,995. The XEi, with equipment levels more on a par with the Grand Vitara, came in at just under £20k. That was almost £4,000 more than the Suzuki, yet the Land Rover could offer nothing more than a 1.8-litre four-cylinder 'K-series' engine compared with the Grand Vitara's silkily smooth V6. It would be some time before Land Rover could finally give the Freelander V6 power, although again that would be a much more expensive vehicle than the price-busting Suzuki.

Decent axle articulation (thanks to the coil-sprung suspension set-up) helped the Grand Vitara when it came to the really rough stuff. This five-door Turbo Diesel was put well and truly through its paces for *4x4 Mart* **magazine.** *(Author)*

Despite its quickly gained market dominance, the Freelander was by no means the only rival to the new Grand Vitara in 1998. Honda's 2.0-litre CR-V had achieved critical acclaim and was attracting a loyal following, with British prices ranging from £16,425 to £17,625. The Kia Sportage – again with just four-cylinder power – offered a good range of different versions, with prices (£14,429 to £19,739) to suit most pockets. The Toyota RAV4 five-door was a tempting buy at £17,749 for the cheapest 2.0 GX, even if it did lack the 'funkiness' of the three-door model. Also, the Subaru Forester 2.0 GLS (£16,400) was a sound choice for anybody who wanted a vehicle that looked more like an estate car than an off-roader.

Within a couple of years, the competition would become even fiercer, thanks to the introduction of the Mitsubishi Shogun Pinin, but for now, the Grand Vitara 2.5 V6 had quite enough rivals to be dealing with.

Fortunately for Suzuki, the Grand Vitara was a good enough vehicle to get the motoring press on its side straight away. Even Britain's *Car* magazine, famous for its bluntness and its often-scathing comments, was impressed with this big-engined new

Suzuki. Mark Walton, reporting from the newcomer's launch in Germany at the Nürburgring, said: 'The 2.5 V6 is very useful. Producing 142bhp and 153lb ft of torque at just 3,500rpm, it's smooth and strong at low revs, and it sweeps the Grand [Vitara] along surprisingly swiftly.'

Car, rarely a magazine renowned for its love of 4x4s and SUVs, even went on to say: 'The whole experience is immensely relaxing and strangely peaceful for a vehicle that purports to be a workhorse, first and foremost.' Praise indeed.

Traditional values

So just what was it that made the new Suzuki Grand Vitara a vehicle that deserved all the praise that it got? There has to be more to a good new car than just a great engine if it is to prove a commercial success. Happily, this biggest of all Suzuki 4x4s was impressive in almost every respect.

Impressive, but not adventurous. Suzuki wisely stuck with their various tried and tested formulae when designing the new Grand Vitara: separate steel chassis; part-time four-wheel drive; dual-range transfer box;

an emphasis on a conservative layout, although this time combined with oodles of equipment and a powerful new engine. As with every other Suzuki of the previous twenty years, the company managed to get the balance of specification versus value for money just about right.

It would have been easy for other manufacturers to criticise Suzuki for retaining the traditional separate-chassis concept – particularly as many were starting to dabble with monocoque construction methods for their own off-roaders, but Suzuki knew best. When Land Rover launched the monocoque-designed Freelander, after a lifetime of using separate chassis for their other vehicles, they soon got themselves into trouble.

Very early examples of the Freelander were reportedly suffering a 'flex' problem, a situation that brought some worryingly negative publicity for the management at

A Grand Vitara doing what it does best: getting dirty and working hard, all without protest. Motoring author Frank Westworth is photographed trying out a 2001-model five-door in rural Shropshire. *(Rowena Hoseason)*

Solihull. 'Land Rover was first made aware of the issue when an owner got a wheel stuck in a drain and could not open the driver's door', reported *Autocar* magazine on 23 September 1998.

Autocar continued, quoting their own anonymous sources: 'Flexing of the 4x4's monocoque body at extreme wheel articulation can prevent the doors from opening, they say. Monocoque designs are less rigid than the ladder frame chassis traditionally used on heavy duty 4x4s.'

Land Rover subsequently solved the problem with some extra strengthening, while simultaneously preparing and modifying the bodyshell for the launch of the forthcoming new V6 version. How the good folk at Suzuki must have been laughing into their sushi.

This, though, is a dilemma that has increasingly faced 4x4 designers over the last decade: monocoque versus chassis? It's a tough call. The former usually results in a smoother on-road ride and superior on-tarmac handling and roadholding, while the latter means

rigidity, strength and a generally better off-road performance.

With most buyers of brand-new 4x4s and SUVs rarely venturing off-road, you can understand any car designer's instinct to go down the monocoque route. For many owners though, it is important for them to know their vehicles are really impressive in the rough, even if they never actually put the theory into practice themselves.

Much to the annoyance of old-school off-roaders everywhere, it appears the vast majority of future 4x4s will be monocoque in design. No doubt most car makers have learned a lesson from the unfortunate experience of those early Freelanders, and monocoque-bodied off-roaders of the 21st century are indeed more rigid than that. But for many enthusiasts, there is nothing quite like a separate-chassis 4x4 when it comes to ultimate off-road capabilities, and, at the time of writing, Suzuki are still very much in agreement.

Big and powerful

When the five-door Grand Vitara 2.5 V6 was launched in Europe in March 1998, there was little indication at that stage that a three-door short-wheelbase was waiting in

In long-wheelbase form, the Grand Vitara offered more luggage space than had ever been seen before in a passenger-carrying Suzuki 4x4. As a family car, this Japanese newcomer caused few complaints. *(Author)*

'The existing Vitara will continue to be built in Spain with a 1.6-litre engine, and it will still be imported to the UK, but in three-door form only. Meanwhile, the Japanese-built Grand Vitara takes over as Suzuki's flagship 4x4, and (limited as ever by the Japanese import quota) Suzuki UK will be bringing in around 3,500 units each year. They shouldn't have any difficulty selling them all, not least because they represent such excellent value for money.' *(Car, June 1998)*

the wings. In fact, as far as most onlookers were concerned, the five-door V6 was simply a new range-topping Suzuki to replace the old five-door 2.0-litre Vitara V6. And that's exactly what it did, with the long-wheelbase old-style Vitara remaining on sale in the UK solely in turbo-diesel guise for a while.

Beneath the newcomer's bonnet sat Suzuki's most powerful engine ever fitted to one of its 4x4s – and what a superb powerplant it was – and still is. A development of the old 2.0-litre V6 that first saw the light of day in the long-wheelbase original Vitara, it now boasted a capacity of 2,493cc. This twin-cam, 24-valve design –

with a class-leading output of 142bhp at 6,200rpm – came with multi-point fuel-injection as standard. It also produced a torque figure of 153lb ft at 3,500rpm – very respectable indeed by petrol-engine standards.

Then, of course, there was the V6's economy. Ah yes; now this is where any large-capacity V6 engine will usually prove rather less impressive, and the Grand Vitara was no exception. Having said that, despite this being a bigger engine in a bigger vehicle, the 2.5-litre Grand Vitara was barely less economical than the 2.0-litre Vitara we had seen before. On the 'Urban' course, the V6 Grand Vitara suffered the indignity of just 21.6mpg as an official figure, but on the 'Combined' cycle, which is generally accepted as a more accurate idea of what you can expect in everyday use, it managed a more respectable 26.6mpg in manual guise and 24.6mpg as an automatic.

In many ways, it was the automatic version of the Grand Vitara V6 that made the most sense. The four-

This was initially the only engine available in the Grand Vitara: the 2.5-litre V6 that has been praised so much for its smoothness, refinement and sheer power. It was the most refined 4x4 that Suzuki had created up until 1998. *(Frank Westworth)*

speed auto seemed to suit the big V6 engine's effortless performance so well; it also meant the fantastic engine wasn't in any way spoiled by the manual version's fairly 'rubbery' gear change. The electronically controlled auto transmission was itself impressive, offering a choice of 'normal' or 'power' modes at the flick of a switch, as well as the lock-up facility first seen on the old Vitara automatics.

Whichever version of Grand Vitara you chose, you were unlikely to be disappointed by the V6's power and performance. The top speed was a healthy 105mph while the 0–60mph sprint time was positively athletic by 4x4 standards, at just 11.6 seconds for the manual model. It made other similarly priced petrol-engined 4x4s feel tortoise-like by comparison.

As you'd expect in a Suzuki of this size and class, the Grand Vitara came as standard with power-assisted rack-and-pinion steering, as well as ventilated disc brakes (front only; the rear still comprised a drum set-

Finally replacing the old diesel-engined Vitara was the Grand Vitara 2.0 Turbo Diesel. What it lacked in outright power it made up for in economy and torque levels. For off-roading, this was the Grand Vitara of choice. *(Author)*

up) to ensure swift, safe stopping from any speed.

Handling was surprisingly impressive to anybody more used to Suzuki's original, far-from-sophisticated products. Like the Vitara before, the new Grand Vitara used independent coil-sprung suspension – and used it to maximum effect. It was good enough to give the newcomer the axle articulation and sheer versatility it needed in order to be a genuinely competent off-roader; and it was supple enough to give a smooth ride with – by class standards – decent on-tarmac handling characteristics.

The Grand Vitara's part-time all-wheel-drive system had grown up too, in line with what other manufacturers were offering. It was now called Suzuki's Drive Select 4x4 set-up, its biggest difference being that the driver could select high-ratio four-wheel drive (from two-wheel drive) while moving in a straight line at

Suzuki hasn't missed out when it comes to 'special edition' Grand Vitaras. Shown here is the well-equipped five-door Limited from the summer of 2000. Smart and classy, don't you think? *(Suzuki GB)*

speeds of up to 62mph. This was done simply by pressing a dashboard-mounted button; the driver could then go from high- to low-ratio all-wheel drive via a more traditional transfer-box lever.

Buyers who demanded even more in the way of gadgets and gizmos weren't disappointed either. All Grand Vitara V6s came with electric windows all round, central locking, electric door mirrors, a CD player, height-adjustable steering wheel, twin airbags, green-tinted glass, the obligatory cup holders, and lots more. Extra-cost options included ABS, air conditioning and an electric sunroof – enough to make an early Freelander feel downright bare by comparison.

The frugal diesel

With the V6 successfully launched and motoring pundits of the time suitably impressed with its capabilities and value for money, Suzuki turned its attention to extra derivatives – the first of which, the 2.0-litre Turbo Diesel, went on sale in Britain in October 1998.

In appearance, equipment and specification, the diesel-powered Grand Vitara was almost identical to its V6 'big brother', but under the bonnet sat the very latest version of Suzuki's 1,998cc intercooled turbo-diesel engine from the Vitara days. Power was adequate rather than outstanding for a diesel engine of this size, thanks

to an output of 86bhp at 4,000rpm. Torque was another matter, with a very generous 159.3lb ft of 'pulling power' at an impressively low 2,000rpm.

Compared with the V6, the Turbo Diesel's performance was probably best described as 'leisurely', but that was to be expected. In an effort to appeal to all kinds of potential buyers, there was even a Turbo Diesel with automatic transmission available – a vehicle with all the get-up-and-go of an elderly sloth.

None of that mattered though, once you had experienced the latest Grand Vitara off-road for the first time. In low-ratio four-wheel drive, here was an even more capable rough-terrain vehicle than the V6, thanks to all that low-down torque and, in typical diesel style, excellent engine braking. In low-ratio first or second gear, your diesel-powered Grand Vitara would plod its way round any off-road course all day, tackling deep mud, steep inclines, massive ruts and unmade tracks galore with seemingly no effort. Select the right gear at the right ratio and just let the vehicle do everything for you – it was a surprisingly fun experience.

Opposite, top: The British International Motor Show of 1998 saw the European launch of the GV range of short-wheelbase, three-door Grand Vitaras. GV1600 and GV2000 models were aimed at a younger market – and again, value-for-money was a high priority, with both GVs seriously undercutting three-door Land Rover Freelanders on price. (Suzuki GB)

Opposite, bottom: Launched at the same time as the Hard Top GV models was what Suzuki officially called the Canvas Top. While the steel-roofed versions were built in Japan, the open-top models were of Canadian manufacture thanks to a joint venture with General Motors of Canada. This was the first vehicle from that venture to be officially sold in the UK. (Suzuki GB)

Below, right: The cheapest model in the Grand Vitara range is the GV1600, shown here in Hard Top guise. Even by 2004, this version cost a very reasonable £11,995, although some Suzuki dealers were selling brand-new ones for £2,000 less. Even the cheapest Freelanders and RAV4s looked distinctly overpriced by comparison. (Author)

Perhaps rather strangely, the Grand Vitara 2.0 Turbo Diesel went on sale in the UK at a slightly higher price than the V6 – £16,775 as a manual, or £17,725 in automatic form. You could spend up to £19,225 on your new Grand Vitara though, if you opted for an automatic Turbo Diesel with the optional package of air conditioning and ABS. It was the first time ever that Suzuki had sold a 4x4 in Europe that was fast approaching £20,000 in price. This was a whole new sector for Japan's most innovative all-wheel drive manufacturer.

Honey, I shrunk the Suzuki

When Suzuki announced they would be launching a short-wheelbase three-door version of the Grand Vitara for 1999, most onlookers agreed it meant the beginning of the end for the original Vitara. Indeed, as various different versions of the compact new short-wheelbase Grand Vitara trickled on to the market, the future for the original Vitara was increasingly uncertain. As covered in the previous chapter, the final UK sales of the (passenger-carrying) Vitara occurred in 2000.

The fact that Suzuki chose the 1998 British International Motor Show – taking place in October – for the European launch of the three-door Grand Vitara says a lot about how important the UK market is for the marque. Britain's motor shows aren't renowned for attracting European launches of any kind, with most manufacturers opting for higher-profile venues such as Geneva or Paris, but for Suzuki in 1998, Birmingham was the one…

Sales weren't due to start until the beginning of '99, but orders were being taken straight away – and interest was high. This was the first brand-new three-door Suzuki 4x4 in a decade, and existing Suzuki owners were keen to see just how good it was.

The contrast between the short-wheelbase Grand Vitara and the original Vitara was considerable. Where the original was sharp and angular, the newcomer was softer, rounder and more in tune with the automotive styling of the late '90s. It gained vital centimetres where they were needed too; in fact, the new model was a useful 250mm longer and 65mm wider than the old-style Vitara short-wheelbase, which again had a knock-on effect when it came to spaciousness and driving dynamics.

Two different engines were on offer to begin with, comprising 1,590cc and 1,995cc 16-valve OHC units with multi-point fuel-injection. These developed 92bhp and 126bhp respectively, which at least ensured lively

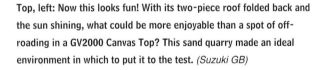

Top, left: Now this looks fun! With its two-piece roof folded back and the sun shining, what could be more enjoyable than a spot of off-roading in a GV2000 Canvas Top? This sand quarry made an ideal environment in which to put it to the test. (Suzuki GB)

Top, right: If you're not a particularly adventurous off-roader, but like the idea of a gentle challenge, you'll find any Grand Vitara makes a superb vehicle in which to tackle green lanes and tracks. Obviously though, only genuine rights of way should be used, and any such routes should be tackled with care. (Author)

Above: This 1999 GV2000 Soft Top really looks the part, thanks to a few important add-ons: smart new alloys, chrome front grille and pedestrian-friendly bull bar. (Suzuki GB)

acceleration and a fun and energetic driving style. To differentiate the short-wheelbase Grand Vitara from its five-door 'big brother', the new models became known, logically enough, as the GV1600 and GV2000; model names which were much more in tune with the three-door's more youthful appeal.

Both the GV1600 and GV2000 were available with either five-speed manual or four-speed automatic transmission – the same gearboxes on offer elsewhere in the Grand Vitara range. The auto in particular was surprisingly enjoyable to drive; I remember road testing a GV2000 Automatic for *4x4 Mart* magazine in 1999, and was bowled over by just how quick and fun-to-drive the vehicle was. Every time I got behind the wheel, I was smiling from ear to ear. Needless to say, it received a very positive write-up.

The author has driven his fair share of Grand Vitaras over the years, usually on test for various magazines or newspapers. The false numberplates are a bit of a giveaway on this occasion! *(Author)*

To maximise the GV's potential, it was available from launch in both three-door Hard Top and two-door Canvas Top guises, to give them their official monikers. This is where things became interesting, because the Hard Top – just like all the five-door Grand Vitaras – was built in and imported from Japan, while the Canvas Top was actually a product of Canada. This was all thanks to yet another deal that Suzuki had going, this time with General Motors of Canada. Between them, the two companies jointly owned CAMI Automotive Inc., a 50/50 venture that had been set up way back in 1986. Almost 13 years on, the UK was finally starting to receive its first supplies of Canadian-built Suzukis.

Like the Spanish-built SJs and Vitaras seen before, this was a neat and effective way of getting round the voluntary import quota that had been levied against Japanese cars since the 1970s. Much to the delight of companies like Suzuki though, this arrangement was finally due to end in 2000, which meant they could bring as many vehicles over from Japan as they could reasonably expect to sell – at long last.

The GV1600 and GV2000 – in both Hard Top and Canvas Top forms – got off to a good start throughout Europe, and soon became a popular choice amongst those who didn't necessarily need the space or versatility of the longer-wheelbase five-door. Buyers

The Grand Vitara's original-style dashboard was clean, uncluttered and ergonomically sound. It was also lacking in modernity or trendiness compared with the Toyota RAV4's. Happily, most potential buyers didn't seem bothered. *(Suzuki GB)*

tended to be younger than for the bigger models, although once again, Suzuki made the mistake of using an interior that was just too bland.

There was nothing intrinsically wrong with the dashboard design of any of the Grand Vitaras, a design that was shared by all models. It was ergonomically good, it did its job and it was easy to understand, but it was also dull looking compared with a Toyota RAV4's. Young buyers attracted by the trendy, 'funky' and imaginative interior of a RAV4 would have been left uninspired once aboard a Suzuki Grand Vitara. Thankfully though, by 2003 Suzuki had realised the error of its ways and, as part of a series of otherwise fairly minor enhancements, finally gave all Grand Vitara models the more modern dashboard they deserved.

One area that was a drastic improvement over previous Suzukis, of course, was that of refinement. Compared with any short-wheelbase Vitara, the GV models offered a massively smoother ride, better handling, greater roadholding, less engine noise, less road roar and an all-round more cosseting

experience. All of which was very necessary if the GVs were to compete with the best of their rivals in the 21st century.

More engines, more choice

That the short-wheelbase GVs and the long-wheelbase Grand Vitaras were technically almost identical was a logical decision. The same 4x4 set-up; same suspension; same transmissions; same almost everything, apart from engines – to begin with, anyway.

With the Grand Vitara offering 2.5 V6 or 2.0 turbo-diesel, and the GV offering 1.6 and 2.0 petrol options, it was inevitable that Suzuki would intro-duce a bit of a crossover, and they did. The 1.6 was always deemed too small for UK-spec Grand Vitaras, so that stayed put in the GV1600. But the

WHAT SUZUKI SAID: The GV2000

'Whoever you are, the GV2000 is about one thing – fun. The stylish, chunky good looks and colour-keyed lower body sections clothe a ladder chassis, selectable four-wheel drive and a powerful 2.0-litre, 16-valve fuel-injected engine. This is a real 4x4 that gives you the freedom and individuality that people have come to expect from Suzuki.'

The biggest off-road Suzuki ever made, as well as being the firm's first seven-seater, was the XL-7 and, in typical Suzuki style, it undercut on price every other seven-seater 4x4 when launched in 2001. *(Suzuki GB)*

1,995cc, 126bhp twin-cam lump was ideal, proving the perfect choice for those buyers who wanted five-door practicality combined with a less thirsty petrol engine. Inevitably too, the Grand Vitara's 1,998cc turbo-diesel would find its way into the smaller GV models.

The Grand Vitara range was just about complete. At last, here was a full line-up of stylish, practical, great value-for-money SUVs with a choice of wheelbases and body styles to suit all tastes. And it was bang up to date, too. Against the increasingly tough competition of a steadily expanding range of Land Rover Freelanders, Suzuki could congratulate themselves on a job well done.

Room for seven?

Suzuki has never been known for complacency. That's why it was considered that there was just one more version of the Grand Vitara which should be introduced, boasting yet another completely new body style. This was the five-door, seven-seater Grand Vitara XL-7 which went on sale in Europe in 2001.

Comprising the front end of a 'normal' Grand Vitara five-door, combined with a longer, slightly more angular looking rump, the newcomer measured 500mm more than the previously biggest version in overall length. This was enough to squeeze in an extra

seat for two in the rear, transforming this particular Grand Vitara into the cheapest seven-seater 4x4 on the market, which it still is today. Costing £17,995 in V6 form by 2003, the Suzuki was drastically undercutting other seven-seaters like the Land Rover Discovery 4.0 V8 GS (£29,340). The Discovery of the time may have been a bigger vehicle with a bigger engine, but was it worth £11,000-plus more than the Suzuki? Land Rover fans would doubtless say yes, but Suzuki fans knew a bargain when they saw it.

WHAT THE PRESS SAID:

'The XL-7 is a logical ultimate progression of Suzuki's mini-off-roader concept. The Vitara was a cheeky fun vehicle aimed at youngsters who'd enjoyed the SJ and Santana experience but wanted something a little more comfortable and practical. The Grand Vitara in its turn appealed to those who'd outgrown the off-road funster Vitara and needed a more sensible and sedate family car. The XL-7 is so sensible there's very little fun factor left ...' *(4x4, September 2003)*

The XL-7 was a useful, 500mm longer than the standard five-door Grand Vitara. To avoid any overlap in the range though, its arrival meant the end of the road for the original Grand Vitara 2.5 V6 – a vehicle which would become redundant once a five-seater version of the XL-7 eventually arrived. *(Suzuki GB)*

The XL-7 was a good drive, too. Power came from a new 2.7-litre quad-cam version of Suzuki's well-proven V6, a powerful and torquey engine at 170bhp and 170lb ft respectively (later raised to 181bhp and 184.4lb ft). A diesel-engined version was also to join the range, powered by the same 2.0-litre turbocharged and intercooler unit found in the Grand Vitara TD.

The equipment levels of the XL-7 were high, with air conditioning, electric windows, central locking, CD player, ABS, dual airbags and alloys all standard.

The XL-7 was not the most fun or 'funky' member of the Grand Vitara family, but it filled a useful niche and offered fantastic value. It wasn't quite such an impressive off-roader, mainly due to its bigger rear overhang; but it would give most rivals a run for their money in the rough.

So why don't we see more XL-7s around now? Because it was always going to be a niche model, aimed at a smaller market than the rest of the Grand Vitara line-up, but I can't help admiring Suzuki though, for spotting yet another gap in the market and exploiting it with a genuine value-for-money product.

Chapter Five

Jimny: back to basics

With Suzuki trying to cover as many different sectors of the off-road market as possible, it was only a matter of time before they got round to designing an SJ for the new Millennium. And that's just what happened in October 1998 with the European debut of the chic and cheerful new Japanese-built Jimny.

Suzuki's move upmarket was being well catered for by the five-door Grand Vitara launched earlier the same year, but with the Samurai now discontinued in many European markets there was an undeniable gap on the bottom rung of the 4x4 ladder. A look at exactly what was on offer from Suzuki in 1998, just prior to the Jimny's announcement proves the point.

The top end of the 'compact SUV' market was well catered for by V6 and Turbo Diesel Grand Vitaras, ranging in price from £16,370 to £17,725, depending on exact specification. A 'mid-range' choice was there too, in thc shape of the short-wheelbase Vitara JX and 4u models, priced from £11,095 to £11,995. Both of these very distinct model ranges were doing extremely well in

City car or 4x4? Suzuki was keen to promote their new-for-1998 Jimny as both. 'Smart in city, tough in nature' was the clever and successful launch slogan. *(Suzuki GB)*

Above: Let's not forget that for all its diminutive dimensions, the Jimny could actually venture away from tarmac and on to rather more challenging terrain. It was as much of an off-roader as any of its predecessors, but rather more refined and sophisticated in the process. *(Suzuki GB)*

Opposite, top: Well, the production Jimny didn't actually end up looking like this early prototype sketch – but you can certainly see some of its styling influences in the end product. What a shame Suzuki never saw fit to build a 'radical' Jimny like this one! *(Suzuki GB)*

Opposite, bottom: An early example of a UK-spec Jimny, on test by the author for *4x4 Mart* magazine in January 1999. For what was a very narrow car, its 'stance' and track looked surprisingly wide. *(Author)*

terms of sales, helping Suzuki to break all records, but for those people who couldn't afford in excess of £11k for a brand-new 4x4, Suzuki no longer had anything to offer. The cupboard was bare.

This was undeniably a serious situation. Admittedly, the 4x4 market had 'grown up' over the years, and better-equipped and more expensive vehicles were in demand, but Suzuki had built its reputation on offering cheap, cheerful and versatile 4x4s – and as far as British buyers were concerned, this had ceased to be the case.

What the company really needed was a sub-£10,000 4x4 to take over from where the old SJ and Samurai had left off. A livelier, more refined, better-equipped, fun-to-drive SJ for modern times – and that is exactly what they got when, on 20 October 1998, the UK market saw the introduction of the long-awaited Jimny.

Back at the bottom

The Jimny name itself wasn't new. The earliest Japanese-spec versions of the old 1970s LJ series were badged as Jimnys, but not when it came to European markets. In any case, this latest incarnation

Like the SJ before it, the Jimny boasted a big, wide-opening, side-hinged rear door – ideal for large loads or for squeezing in the weekly shopping. Suzuki had to think of the everyday needs of its potential customers more than ever in the 1990s. *(Author)*

of the Jimny was a world away from those early examples.

Still, you only had to glance at the 1998 Jimny to see hints of Suzuki's heritage in there. Like the SJ and Samurai before, the Jimny was tall and upright, but this time with a 'chunkiness' that seemed to give it a whole new character of its own. Flared wheelarches, big body-coloured bumpers, neat roof rails and a large glass area made sure the stylish little Jimny looked bang up to date.

If the Jimny had all the styling characteristics of a full-size SUV, it certainly didn't have the stature or dimensions. At just 3,625mm in length and a mere 1,600mm in width, the Jimny was small enough to fit into just about any inner city parking space and was

manoeuvrable enough to power its way through even the densest of traffic situations. No wonder Suzuki boasted that Jimny was '… the business in the city'.

The timing of the Jimny's launch couldn't have been better. The late 1990s saw a resurgence in sales of small cars, a trend that has continued through the early years of the 21st century. There has been a similar major increase in sales of 4x4s, too, so surely the smallest new 4x4 on sale in Europe couldn't fail … could it?

To succeed, the Jimny had to be good. Very good indeed. Gone were the days when awkward handling characteristics or a complete lack of refinement would be acceptable in any small car. The Jimny not only had

WHAT SUZUKI SAID: The Jimny Range

'Jimny – tough enough to explore the wild life in the city or the country. A car that, like you, is like no other. Estate or Soft Top, the 1.3-litre Jimny is a real 4x4 with real character.'

to be a massive step forward from the Samurai it was effectively replacing; it also had to compete with the sophisticated new Renault Clios, Volkswagen Polos and Fiat Puntos that were proving so popular. The Jimny had to appeal not just to 4x4 fans but to the kind of folk who would otherwise go out and buy a top-class 'supermini'.

There was certainly no doubting the Jimny's value for money. At just £9,995 for the 1.3 JLX with manual transmission (the four-speed auto cost £875 more), the hard-top Jimny was in the same price bracket as the Ford Ka3 (£9,820), Citroën Saxo 1.4 SX (£10,000) and Vauxhall Corsa 1.4 LS (£9,610) – three cars that tended to be bought by those looking for fun and economy.

That the Jimny's main rivals were front-wheel-drive hatchbacks says a lot about the state of the 4x4 market in '98. There was simply no other 'proper' 4x4 at less than £10,000 any more. The Fiat Panda 4x4 was long since dead; imports of the Lada Niva had ceased the previous year, and Daihatsu's new Terios model was grossly overpriced upon its launch, with even the cheapest costing £12,205. The Jimny was, quite simply, in a class of its own.

That situation wouldn't remain forever though. By 2003, and with different importers now in charge of Daihatsu, the five-door Terios range started at a far more sensible £10,495 for the 1.3 Tracker model. A sound buy now? Well, perhaps; after all, the Terios offered permanent four-wheel drive and five-door versatility, both lacking from the diminutive Jimny. On the other hand, the Terios had an ungainly appearance (too tall for its width … or too narrow for its height?) and simply wasn't in the same league as the Suzuki when it came to off-road abilities. No wonder the Jimny has consistently outsold the Daihatsu Terios every year since both models went on sale in 1998.

Conventional fun

In line with the rest of the Suzuki 4x4 range, the new Jimny was conventional in its layout and specification: ladder-frame chassis; part-time all-wheel drive; dual-range transfer box; everything pretty much as before.

One big development since the days of the Samurai though, was the adoption of what Suzuki called its Drive Action 4x4 set-up. As with the Grand Vitara, this allowed the driver to switch from rear-wheel drive to high-ratio four-wheel drive at speeds of up to 62mph. Bring the car to a halt and you could then switch to low-ratio all-wheel drive if the going got really tough. It all added to the convenience of the Jimny, without

Simple but effective is probably the best way to describe the Jimny's dashboard. For such a small vehicle, its whole interior looked surprisingly 'grown up'. Equipment levels were high too, all versions coming with electric front windows, central locking, CD player and electrically adjustable door mirrors. *(Author)*

WHAT SUZUKI SAID: The Jimny 1.3 JLX

The young, and the young at heart, will enjoy the many features of this exciting new 4x4 vehicle. The 16-valve 1.3-litre engine size provides spirited performance, reliability and dependability in an all-round package that brings quality with a sense of fun within the reach of a wide cross-section of consumers.'

As with most Suzuki 4x4s, the Jimny's standard boot space is limited. Fold the split/fold rear seat though, and you have a two or three-seater vehicle with a useful amount of load area. In fact, with the back seat fully down, the Jimny almost seems to take on the role of a small van. *(Author)*

proving over-complicated or technically difficult.

Beneath the bonnet of the Jimny sat the latest version of Suzuki's lively 1,298cc OHC four-cylinder engine, albeit with 16-valve head and multi-point fuel-injection as standard. This meant a very healthy output of 79bhp at 6,000rpm, with a perfectly reasonable 76.7lb ft of torque at 4,500rpm. It was all a sign of just how far things had moved on since the launch of the original Vitara ten years earlier; the 1.6-litre Vitara was actually less powerful (75bhp) in its original form than the 1.3-litre Jimny of 1998.

Linked to either a five-speed manual or four-speed automatic transmission, the Jimny's powerplant proved lively in operation. A top speed of 88mph and 0–60mph time of around 16 seconds didn't sound spectacular, but in practice the car felt sprightly and was able to keep up easily with the traffic around it.

One minor letdown was the 'notchiness' of the Jimny's manual gear change. It certainly improves with increased mileage, but it could never be described as slick.

In every other respect, the Jimny's mechanical design and layout was a joy. Power-assisted steering came as standard (albeit the old recirculating ball-and-nut system), as did front disc brakes. The flexible all-coil suspension set-up offered a fairly jittery ride over poor road surfaces, but came into its own in off-road situations where its impressive travel was extremely useful.

Being such a small vehicle with a short wheelbase, the Jimny had just the right dimensions to make the

WHAT THE PRESS SAID:

'We remember how the old SJ series was compared with bigger 4x4s. We recall the uncomfortably choppy ride, the dodgy handling and the basically uninspiring dynamics. Ah yes, we remember it all well. Which is why the Jimny came across to us as something of a revelation: this little Suzuki goes round corners pretty well. Shock, horror! Hold the front page!' (4x4 Mart, January 2000)

most of its off-road promise. Approach and departure angles of 42° and 46° respectively were highly useful, while the ground clearance of 190mm was quite adequate for most situations. But did all this actually make the Jimny an impressive off-road machine in practice? Find out a bit further on …

A major feature of the Jimny, like all previous small

The Jimny **Soft Top** looked great when it arrived in March **2000**, just in time for that year's summer. Disappointment came though, when the motoring press discovered just how difficult it was to remove and then refit the convertible's rear roof section. Surely Suzuki could have developed a more user-friendly system? *(Suzuki GB)*

Suzukis of course, was the likelihood of low running costs. It was certainly cheap to buy, which obviously got things off to a good start. Economy of 35–39mpg in most owners' hands was acceptable if not spectacular for a small, 1.3-litre car. Likewise, an insurance rating of Group 7 was affordable for most, even though a good many 'superminis' came in two or three groups lower than that.

But there is another aspect to running costs that is often overlooked – and that is the question of reliability. With its three-year/60,000-mile warranty (matching the rest of the Suzuki line-up of the time), any owner of a new Jimny must have felt a certain reassurance; and if the Jimny were to prove to be as reliable and trouble-free as all its predecessors (which it would), there could be few unexpected expenses later on.

The top comes off

With Suzuki's tradition of introducing fabric-roofed versions of all its 4x4s over the years, it was only a matter of time before the Jimny would follow suit. This finally took place in March 2000 when the logically named Jimny Soft Top arrived from Spain, well in time for the summer.

With the hood down, the newcomer looked terrific. As with the GV models, the Jimny's fabric roof came in two sections. The section over the front of the cab was easy to remove, which made it great for a spot of

instant fresh air when the mood took you. Rolled up and stowed in the Jimny's little boot area, it was trouble-free.

Then, though, there was the rear section to contend with. I remember complaining about this in a road test I did for *4x4 Mart* magazine, just after the model's launch:

'By the time you've unzipped the sides and removed them, likewise with the rear window, and then unclipped the hood itself and folded it down and out of sight, a good two or three minutes have passed. And getting the thing back up again, including mating all the zips together that hold the various separate sections in place, takes even longer – which can be frustrating if you're stuck at the side of the road in the midst of an unexpected rain storm.

'That's all a bit of a shame, because with the hood down the Jimny Soft Top actually looks good and turns heads everywhere it goes. Everyone seems to love it. If

Top down, the sun shining and a deserted open road ahead of you – the finest way to enjoy the cute but flawed Jimny Soft Top. In the UK, this was the cheapest new convertible you could buy, which no doubt helped it to enjoy healthy sales from day one. *(Suzuki GB)*

only Suzuki could come up with some method of making the rear hood removal a one-stage operation, then this would be a superb set-up.'

It was such a letdown. The Jimny Soft Top looked great and seemed to make a lot of sense – on paper. But for anybody who fancied some inexpensive wind-in-the-hair fun, the whole process of getting the roof off and back on again was just too much of a chore.

There was certainly no knocking the Soft Top's value though. Sold at exactly the same price as the hard-top JLX, it was by far the cheapest convertible on sale in the UK. The only rag-top vehicle that managed to undercut it on price in Continental Europe was the latest version of the evergreen Samurai. Suzuki really had cornered the market in value-for-money open-air motoring.

Money where my mouth is

As if to prove the economics of buying a brand-new Jimny, I did just that myself back in July 2003. I was after an affordable new 4x4 for personal use and was seriously considering both the Jimny and the Daihatsu Terios as possibilities.

I arrived at the conclusion that the Jimny was the best option of the two without much difficulty. I have always preferred the Suzuki's chunky styling to the Terios's strangely narrow and upright stance as well as the Jimny's driving style, having piloted several examples of both vehicles extensively over the years. I also rated the Jimny's off-road prowess higher than the Terios', thanks to its shorter wheelbase, old-fashioned dual-range transfer box and high ground clearance. But could I justify spending the best part of £10,000?

Then something happened; I was leafing through my local free newspaper when I noticed an advert for one of the three Suzuki dealers that can be found within 12 miles of my home in the Midlands. A brand-new Jimny could be mine, insisted the ad, for a mere £7,495 on the road. That was a full £2,500 less than list price – a discount of 25 per cent. It seemed almost too good to be true, but I grabbed the phone and made the inevitable call.

What was the catch? There wasn't one, it seemed. The vehicle would indeed be brand new. It was an official UK model (not a 'grey' import), it would have no previous owners on its V5 Registration Document, and it would be available almost immediately. In fact, the offer would only be available provided I registered the Jimny during July 2003.

No problem, I thought, and I was seriously tempted. But provisional arrangements to go and pay the Suzuki dealer a visit the next day fell apart when I got tied up with a work project – and, before I knew it, a few more days had passed.

Which was a good job really, because the following Thursday, with the latest edition of the same free local newspaper pushed through my letterbox, another ad for another Suzuki dealer caught my eye. Brand-new Jimnys for £6,995! Or a mere £200 more if I wanted metallic paint. No previous owners; no miles on the clock; the usual three-year warranty; three years' roadside assistance; the lot.

Just like the other Suzuki dealer, this one also insisted the car would have to be bought and registered by the end of July, but that suited me fine. Within half an hour of reading their advert, I had arrived at the showroom and was filling in the paperwork, ready for delivery the following week. I had made up my mind – and there was no stopping me now.

Only two Jimnys remained in stock when I got there – one in 'flat' Antares Red at £6,995, the other in metallic Cyprus Blue at £7,195. I figured it was worth the extra couple of hundred to get what I think is a far nicer hue, and so the blue one was duly reserved for me.

It all seemed to happen so quickly in the end. After what felt like an age of soul-searching about which used 4x4 should be gracing my driveway, there I was placing an order for a brand-new one. And this from a person who has always argued against the economics of buying brand-new cars. It just shows how a generous promotion can tempt even the most hardened cynics amongst us.

Opposite: The author took the plunge in July 2003 when he bought himself a brand-new Jimny 1.3 JLX – a bargain at just over £7k, thanks to generous dealer discounts at the time. He was soon delighted with his purchase. *(Author)*

Below: Suzuki was never afraid to put the Jimny's off-road abilities to the test. Shown here is one of the earliest UK-spec models showing just what it was capable of. Unusually for a small, petrol-engined 4x4, downhill engine braking was actually very impressive. *(Suzuki GB)*

Jimny in the rough

I have always suspected that when it comes to the Jimny vs Daihatsu Terios debate, the Suzuki really is unbeatable in one vital area: off-road prowess. After all, the Terios doesn't even offer a dual-range transfer box for when the going gets really tough.

Having driven examples of both vehicles off-road I decided to prove my point this time round, so I took my very own Jimny along to an organised off-road event to see what it was really made of. The opportunity came courtesy of Richard Walsh of 4x4 Funday Ltd, and the venue was the superb Farley Quarry site at Much Wenlock in Shropshire. This is the kind of site that sorts the men from the boys and is the type of site that would probably leave a Terios stranded up to its axles in mud and slurry.

By the end of the day, I was completely and utterly amazed at just how capable the tiny Suzuki proved to be in the rough – and that's despite me already having fairly high expectations.

All the ingredients are there, of course: short wheelbase; generous ground clearance and a dual-range transfer box. On the other hand, a peppy 1.3-litre petrol engine is traditionally not the ideal off-road powerplant. It is hardly likely to provide the ultimate in downhill engine braking, is it? And, of course, in a brand-new 4x4 that costs well under £10k, we can't expect such luxuries as Land Rover's Hill Descent Control.

Indeed not, and yet, with low-ratio four-wheel drive selected, I found the Jimny really did offer decent engine braking. How? The gearing, it seems, was just right; I was able to ease my way down steep, slippery, muddy slopes in first gear, with the engine keeping everything under control – and with complete confidence at all times. With my feet off both the accelerator and the

The author wasn't afraid to take his own Jimny off-road, as proved by this appearance at an off-road fun day in Shropshire in February 2004. Even so, no standard Jimny could hope to be as accomplished off-road as the mildly modified old Daihatsu Fourtrak that's just passing by... (Author)

brake pedals (obviously), I was able to simply let the car do all the work in such situations.

All of that is familiar, of course, to drivers of more dedicated off-roaders like the diesel-engined Series III Land Rovers which were prevalent on the day. But for the off-road pilot of a petrol-powered shoebox, it was something of a revelation!

The Jimny also proved its worth when powering up steep inclines or when manoeuvring its way through narrow paths with sharp turns when you least expected them. As the day wore on though, and as the number of vehicles taking part increased and the ground became more churned-up and muddy, I wondered whether the Jimny's competence and confidence would continue. It did; in fact, the muddier and trickier the terrain became, the more the Jimny seemed to revel in the experience.

Like all the old SJs that have gone before, the Jimny uses its sheer lack of weight to ensure it doesn't get bogged down. Point it in the direction of a deep 'mud bath' and – unlike the Discoverys, Shoguns and Troopers of this world – the cheeky Suzuki almost seems to 'float' its way over. Keeping the revs up helps, as does maintaining momentum at all times. Achieve both and you will find a humble Jimny a pretty impressive off-road machine.

All of that on standard road tyres too, which made me think seriously about investing in a spare set of wheels shod with off-road rubber, specifically for days like this.

It's a tempting thought as it wouldn't take a lot for any Jimny to become a formidable off-road competitor.

Personal development

It says a lot about the worthiness and success of the original Jimny that, even six years on, it was still relatively unchanged in both style and specification. It also says much about what happened to car prices in Britain between 1998 and 2004, that the original list price of £9,995 remained exactly the same. Six years of inflation, at however low a rate, should logically have seen the price of the Jimny rising slightly. But the

WHAT THE PRESS SAID:

'This is the cheapest 'proper' off-roader in the UK. It drops marks for minimal boot space, tight rear legroom and a bouncy ride, but its compact overall size makes it easy to drive on and off road. The 1.3-litre engine revs like crazy but performance is moderate, although it's flexible enough to wriggle over slippery ground. With short overhangs, a high eye level and automatic transmission option, the Jimny is popular with urban cowboys – and girls – but it's good off-road too.' *(4x4, October 2003)*

Limited editions have come and gone, one of the most popular being the 02 Soft Top from 2002. Two-tone paint and three-spoke alloys certainly made this Jimny stand out from all the others. *(Suzuki GB)*

pressure on car manufacturers throughout the late '90s to bring UK prices more in line with those in Continental Europe resulted in many car prices stabilising during this period. This means, in these early years of the 21st century, the Jimny offers better value than ever before.

A major change to the Jimny line-up was the replacement of its original, well-proven 1,298cc four-pot engine in March 2001 with a new 1,328cc DOHC unit, although only on Japanese-built hard-top versions. Not dissimilar in size or spec (apart from its 'twin cam' set-up), this latest engine did little to change the overall driving style or appeal of the Jimny, other than being slightly more refined at speed and marginally less harsh when worked really hard. Power and torque levels remained more or less as before, with 79bhp available at 5,500rpm and a reasonable 81lb ft of 'pulling power' at 4,500rpm.

Four years from the introduction of the new DOHC engine, the situation is still pretty much the same. The Jimny hard-top models built in Japan employ the new

Opposite, top: Finished in metallic Mars Gold (exclusive to the Hard Top model) and fitted with the same alloys found on an 02 edition Soft Top, this eye-catching Jimny would turn heads in any city centre. *(Suzuki GB)*

Opposite, below: Not to everyone's taste perhaps, but at least this photograph from October 1998 gives an indication of how any Jimny could look if you opted for just about every accessory in the catalogue. The owner of such a vehicle would probably have had floral wallpaper and net curtains at home... *(Suzuki GB)*

powerplant, while Spanish-built (by Suzuki Santana) soft-top versions still have the 1,298cc SOHC engine used right from the start.

Despite the fact that comparatively little about the Jimny has changed since its debut in 1998, a couple of 'limited edition' models have been and gone. The 02 version of the Soft Top arrived in 2002, offering smart two-tone paintwork and a handful of extra goodies for just £500 more than the standard model. While towards the end of 2003, a 'special edition' hard-top model known as the Mode also appeared, with smart alloys, special paint and improved equipment levels,

again at £10,495. Interestingly, the well-equipped Jimny Mode ended up by being made a permanent member of the range in March 2004, such was its popularity.

Even the most basic Jimny though, was never short on equipment and niceties considering its value-for-money pricing. All models came from new with electric front windows, central locking, tinted glass, dual airbags, a CD player and electrically adjustable door mirrors. With a wide range of official Suzuki accessories available – from rear spoilers to front fog lamps; bull bars, to special spare wheel covers – there were lots of options open to owners once they had got their Jimny parked on the driveway.

Suzuki came up with a worthy, likeable and hugely entertaining replacement for the Samurai when it brought the Jimny to the UK and Europe in 1998. Now, several years on, its appeal remains undiminished, and its value for money is greater than ever.

The Jimny's success story continues, several years on from the model's debut way back in 1998. Shown here is a 2004 example, complete with metallic paint and ever-popular three-spoke alloys. The Jimny's styling has remained remarkably fresh and modern looking throughout its career to date. *(Suzuki GB)*

Chapter Six

Choosing your Suzuki

Let's start this chapter by pointing out one obvious, but glorious fact: no matter what your budget is, you are sure to be able to afford a Suzuki 4x4. And that means, whether you have £150 or £15,000 to spend, there's easy access to a whole lot of fun just waiting for you.

Unlike so many other 4x4 manufacturers, Suzuki have always made a point of focusing on the affordable end of the market, from the European launch of the LJ80 in 1978 through to the current model line-up. It's true; at the time of writing, the most expensive Suzuki 4x4 on sale in the UK is the XL-7 2.0 TDI seven-seater at a shade under £20,000. By Suzuki standards, that's a lot of money, and yet, in reality, it means the dearest

example of the marque falls only halfway up the price range of Land Rover's entry-level model, the Freelander. Of course, Land Rover then goes on to offer other vastly more expensive models, some costing in excess of £60,000. See what we mean about value for money?

No matter how impressive a vehicle like the seven-seater Suzuki XL-7 is though, it is not necessarily one that appeals to out-and-out enthusiasts. It's a family

Are you looking for a cheap SJ just for off-road fun? You could pay £150 or less for one with no MoT. Remember though, that for most official off-road fun day events, vehicles need to be road legal and MoT'd, even if they're trailered there. *(Author)*

holdall, a 'people carrier' with the versatility of all-wheel drive; it's not a vehicle you buy for the sheer love of it.

Other Suzukis are different, however. Second-hand models like the SJ series and Vitara, and even brand-new examples of the Jimny and Grand Vitara, are so often bought by folk who are real enthusiasts. They are not necessarily highly experienced in the art of off-roading, nor are they automatically 4x4 owners of longstanding. But they are, in a big majority of cases, the kind of people who choose Suzukis for their sheer fun appeal and for their entertainment value.

Fun-to-drive cars seem to be in such short supply these days. Modern vehicles are, of course, wonderfully competent and vastly superior to their predecessors in so many ways, but one thing they're often not, is fun, amusing, or entertaining. That's a charge you would find difficult to level against any enthusiast's Suzuki 4x4 however, and even if your budget is minuscule by the standards of today, there is still no reason why you can't have more fun behind the wheel than with almost anything else on the road – or off it.

Next to nothing

Even with as little as £150 (or sometimes even less) burning a hole in your pocket, it is possible to enter into the world of all-wheel-drive Suzuki ownership. The downside, of course, is that the vehicle in question is unlikely to be in particularly good condition. In fact, it's unlikely to be able to pass its MoT test. It might not even be a very good runner, but at least it's a start.

At this price level, we're looking at examples of the evergreen SJ range, and of course, not particularly good ones. As we shall see in the next chapter, the SJ isn't immune to problems, perhaps the most serious being rust. Rot, corrosion, call it what you will, it is responsible for killing off thousands of SJs over the years and is the main reason for MoT failure and, ultimately, a one-way trip to the nearest scrap yard. If you are spending as little as £150 on an SJ, it's going to have its fair share of rust; certainly enough to prevent an easy MoT pass.

You might think this isn't too much of a concern. Perhaps you only want a cheap and cheerful SJ that you can put on the back of a trailer, take to the odd off-road fun day, and then enjoy yourself well and truly putting it through its paces. Who cares about some MoT-failing rust with such a vehicle? In fact, who cares about MoTs at all in such circumstances?

SJs, Santanas and Samurais are more likely to rust than most off-road Suzukis, partly because of their age these days. Front wings, wheelarches, doors and chassis sections are particularly prone to corrosion. (Author)

The answer is, the organisers of such events. Even with a non-competitive fun day that any enthusiast can take part in, the organisers normally insist on a vehicle being MoT'd, insured and roadworthy, even if it is trailered there. Bear this in mind when buying, as it may well affect your final choice of vehicle. The exact rules regarding fun days, and where you can go to take part in them, will be covered later.

Of course, it's a different situation if you have your own land on which you just want a Suzuki to 'play

Where can you find the best-value SJ-series vehicles? Local 'free-ad' newspapers are often the best source, and they also crop up quite often on the eBay Internet auction website. *(Author)*

with'. You make your own rules and you take your own risks. Do ensure that the vehicle is basically solid and safe though; if anything goes wrong, or an accident is caused on your own land by something failing on the vehicle, you will only have yourself to blame.

On-road bargains?

Most people buying a cheap and cheerful old SJ will also want to use it on the road. Not necessarily on an everyday basis, but the vehicle will usually need to be roadworthy and reliable enough to ensure it can be driven between off-road courses legally and safely.

Some people, of course, do still use their SJs, Santanas and Samurais every day, although these tend to be folk who don't need to cover 20,000 motorway miles each year. The SJ's drawbacks of limited on-road performance (from the SJ410 anyway), harsh ride quality and less-than-perfect handling characteristics

do not inspire such use. But assuming your annual mileage is reasonably low, your journeys don't last several hours non-stop and you're prepared to put up with an unforgiving ride, you will find any well-maintained SJ an economical and practical every-day machine. They usually prove to be extremely reliable, seem to thrive on hard work, and they are a vastly more interesting 'old banger' than any ancient Ford Fiesta.

So just how much do you need to pay nowadays to get an SJ of some description that has still got a few years of life left in it? Bizarrely, probably more now than you might have done two or three years ago. So popular are these machines as cheap and cheerful introductions to the world of off-roading, they are becoming increasingly sought after. This means the days of 'hundred-quid' MoT'd bargains are fast disappearing.

Much depends, naturally, on where you start looking for an SJ, Santana or Samurai. You still see them cropping up in local newspapers and even on postcards in shop windows from time to time; and these can often be the cheapest sources. For around £300–£500, you

will probably find a 1980s example in solid albeit far from pristine condition.

The same sort of money also sees old SJs selling on the Internet auction website eBay (www.ebay.co.uk), but always bear in mind that you are usually bidding on a vehicle you have not even seen 'in the metal', and you're basically accepting the vendor's description of its condition, mileage and so on without question. Bargains can sometimes be found on such websites, but don't bid without truly satisfying yourself that the vehicle is exactly as described. If in any doubt, go and see the Suzuki before you place an online bid. Always remember that the placing of an eBay (or similar) bid is legally binding; if you win the auction and you then change your mind about buying at the agreed price, the vendor has every right to pursue the matter through legal channels.

AutoTrader can be a good source of cheap Suzukis, but dwindling numbers of SJs means you won't always find what you're looking for straight away. Still, it's worth checking out the company's website (www.autotrader.co.uk) as this will give you an idea

If you're paying just a few hundred pounds for an MoT'd SJ, don't expect it to be in great condition. Soft-top models will usually have worn or torn hoods; bodywork will be showing signs of wear and tear; mechanically though, things should be pretty healthy. *(Author)*

of what's available both nationally and locally.

One of the best sources of affordable SJs is the vast array of different 'free-ad' newspapers published throughout the UK. *Loot* is well known throughout south-east England, while the Birmingham area's *Bargain Pages* is similarly successful, you will probably find there is an equivalent newspaper in your own area and these really do throw up a fascinating range of cars for sale each week. Check them out and you will probably be surprised at just what's available through such sources.

Is bigger better?

Sticking with the 'cheap and cheerful' end of the market for a moment, we can now include the evergreen Suzuki Vitara in this category. As the model has grown older and its original trendiness has faded, so prices have tumbled. All right, so it is still possible to go out and spend anything up to £5,000–£6,000 on a modified, immaculate Vitara from a specialist; equally though, it is now feasible to spend less than £1,000 on an early example, at which price level it becomes a very tempting proposition indeed.

No wonder then, that so many amateur off-road fanatics are now turning to the Vitara rather than the SJ for modifying and enjoying 'in the rough'. The Vitara rusts less, offers more power and has better on-road handling, and yet, thanks to its straightforward layout and simple technical spec, its potential when it comes to off-road modifications is enormous. Nowadays, increasing numbers of modified Vitaras are being seen in off-road competition, often proving more than a match for the bigger, more expensive non-Suzuki opposition.

For serious off-roading, the Vitara of choice has to be a short-wheelbase model. In any rough terrain, the shorter the wheelbase, the less chance of getting 'grounded', particularly if the vehicle has been fitted with raised suspension. It is a fairly simple modification, as described later; yet it endows any three-door Vitara with the kind of ground clearance so necessary when driving away from tarmac.

Other mechanical mods are relatively straightforward with a Vitara, a subject covered in detail in Chapter

Thinking of buying a Vitara? There's perhaps never been a better time than now. Values of older examples have dropped to very affordable levels. A 1989/90 example could be yours for as little as £1,000 these days, but this 'N' registration Soft Top will fetch considerably more due to its excellent condition. *(Frank Westworth)*

Nine. Many of these can be carried out on a fairly tight budget, enabling you to make the most of your off-roading ambitions without spending a fortune.

Terrific on tarmac?

So far in this chapter, I have pointed out the kind of Suzukis that are available for those enthusiasts who want to go off-roading on the cheap. Not everyone who buys a second-hand or well-used Suzuki 4x4 though, is necessarily destined for off-road action. Many people still like the idea of buying a cheap-and-cheerful 4x4 purely for everyday transport, without even a thought for heading off-road. They are attracted by the looks, the get-you-through-any-winter traction, the image and the fun factor. This still applies to healthy numbers of SJ and Vitara buyers, as well as those with slightly larger budgets who are tempted

Long-wheelbase five-door Vitaras aren't the best choice for off-road work as they're more likely to get 'grounded' when the terrain gets particularly tough. For on-road use though, you end up with a lot more useable space and a superior ride quality. It all comes down to what you personally need from your next 4x4. *(Author)*

by the earlier Jimny and Grand Vitara models that are now available in fairly large numbers on the used car market.

I have already mentioned the drawbacks of any SJ model when used every day: the lacklustre performance of the 970cc models, the harsh ride and the 'interesting' handling when pushed to the limit. These are all well-known factors and are part of the SJ's genetic make-up, but at least they give the little car a degree of character; in fact, it's difficult to drive an SJ and not have a broad grin on your face most of the time. (Unless, of course, you're halfway through a 300-mile motorway trip…) With a half-decent, presentable and fully roadworthy SJ or Samurai likely to be yours for anything between £500 and £1,000, we're talking bargain basement motoring here.

At that price level, the SJ isn't so much up against other 4x4s. Instead, it is competing on price with second-hand Escorts, Rover 200s and ancient Astras … the kind of used cars that are about as much fun and as entertaining as a credit card statement. Compared with such 'old bangers', a sub-£1,000 SJ or Samurai offers reliability, economy and major entertainment value, as

Opposite, top: The Jimny has changed remarkably little over the years, as the author's 2003 model illustrates. Early examples from 1998/99 are now extremely affordable, and can often be found at less than £4,000 privately. That's fantastic value for money, as long as it's a well-maintained vehicle in reasonable condition. *(Author)*

Opposite, bottom: It might sound obvious, but the Jimny is a tiny vehicle by modern standards. Are you sure you can manage with a 4x4 of such diminutive proportions? Take a good, long test drive before making your decision. If you need lots of room and a big boot, this isn't the 4x4 for you! *(Author)*

Below: It is still possible to spend a lot of money on a Vitara from a specialist, but you get what you pay for. Top-priced examples in excess of £5,000 tend to have been expensively modified and are in near-perfect condition. If you want the best and are willing to pay for it, companies such as Midlands-based Suzi Q's will oblige. *(Author)*

WHAT THE PRESS SAID – Vitara

'It was a sad day when Suzuki withdrew the much-loved Vitara from the UK market. OK, there weren't crowds of mourners lining the streets of London in any kind of Diana-esque tribute to the little Vit. But many enthusiasts were saddened. And even more were puzzled when faced with the prospect of the bulbous-looking Grand Vitara as the only new alternative to the cool, stylish and full-of-street-cred original Vitara. All right, so the Grand Vitara's been successful. And, yes, it's selling particularly well in Britain. But if Suzuki really thinks it's a trendy and youthful replacement for the baby Vit, the vehicle that literally changed the shape of miniature 4x4s back in 1988, they're surely mistaken.'
(4x4 Mart, January 2003)

does a cheap-and-cheerful Vitara, albeit in a slightly more 'grown up' way.

With an early Vitara, you get a 1.6-litre engine, more space than any SJ, performance that feels positively lively and handling that doesn't cause alarm in an emergency. In fact, compared with a humble little SJ, even an early bog-standard Vitara feels almost sophisticated.

Those who have been used to a comfortable modern hatchback rather than an ageing 4x4 will find the Vitara's ride quality rather choppy and fairly harsh over some surfaces. But compared with other all-wheel drives, the Suzuki is an impressive all-rounder to drive. It feels safe, secure and steady under most conditions. Oh, and it is also likely to suffer from fewer corrosion problems than an SJ.

That is not to say the Vitara is immune from rust; far from it, as we shall discover in Chapter Seven, but it is certainly no worse than most other cars launched at the end of the 1980s – and it is a heck of a lot better than many of them.

At £1,000–£2,000, an early Vitara with an MoT is unlikely to be immaculate, but it should be structurally sound, cosmetically OK, mechanically fine and capable of several more years of reliable, everyday use. Buy a good one at this price level, maintain it well and you could still be using it five years from now. It's a case of finding the very best example you can for your money, and with more Vitaras to choose from on the second-hand market than SJs or Samurais these days, it shouldn't take you too long to find your ideal example.

Moving up the scale

As we start to move slightly higher up the second-hand Suzuki price scale, other models suddenly come into view. However, if your budget is in the region of £3,000–£4,000, you are still very much in Vitara territory.

This kind of money should buy you a very smart five to seven-year-old Vitara with a low mileage and a full service history in its favour. It is likely to have been well looked after, shouldn't be showing any major signs of deterioration and will have a whole wad of paperwork with it to show exactly what has been spent on it over the years. All of this is perfectly reasonable to expect at this price level; if it's not there, simply walk away and start looking at other Vitaras. There are usually plenty of late-model examples to choose from throughout the UK, advertised both privately and by the trade.

At £3,500 to £4,000 though, another Suzuki 4x4 is now within your grasp in the shape of an early

(1998/99) Jimny. Costing just a tad under £10,000 when new, the first of the Jimnys are now a more affordable proposition at around the £4k mark. We have seen examples advertised even cheaper than that, but these tend to have covered a higher-than-average mileage and have been neglected somewhat.

A £4,000 Jimny should still be a smart-looking machine, albeit with a few of the scrapes and grazes one would expect to see on any seven-year-old vehicle. It will be an 'S' or 'T' registration example, probably with 50–60,000 miles on the clock and no more than about three owners so far in its life. If you can tick all these boxes, you are happy with the condition and you think you can live with a 4x4 as small as a Jimny, this could indeed be money well spent.

That last point about the size of the Jimny is a valid one. Since 1998, the model has obviously benefited from being one of the cheapest new 4x4s on the market, and has attracted healthy sales partly as a result of this. But living with a vehicle like a Jimny every day for two or three years will certainly show up any drawbacks, and its small size is sometimes seen as one of these.

Perhaps that is why we tend to see fair numbers of one-year-old Jimnys on the market these days, often on the forecourts of garages that have no connection with Suzuki whatsoever. Some people get tempted by the price of the Jimny and its chunky mini-4x4 looks and promptly place an order. Then when they realise just how restricted the rear legroom can be; how tricky it is to get kids in and out of the back; how small the boot is; how unrefined the Jimny is compared with a similarly-priced new Renault Clio or Citroën C2. Well, that's when they get swayed by the idea of returning to the 'supermini' market, and promptly part-exchange their less-than-a-year-old Jimny for something a bit more convenient. It's true; check out the second-hand Jimnys on garage forecourts in your area and you will see what I mean.

There's nothing intrinsically wrong with the Jimny; after all, I bought a brand-new example myself, and

WHAT THE PRESS SAID – Jimny

'If the Daihatsu Terios has the edge over the Suzuki Jimny in terms of on-road performance, the positions are reversed once we get into the dirt. The traditional high and low ratios in the Jimny's two-speed transfer box mean that rocky stretches of track can be traversed at lower speeds and with less revs than in the Terios.' *(4x4, November 2002)* absolutely raved about it. But I'll be the first to admit that it is not the car for everyone. If you're tempted, make sure you have a good, long test drive before making your decision. If you're anything like me, you will soon fall for the thing and will be writing out a cheque before you have even turned off the engine. But just make sure you can live with one before you take the plunge.

Going for the Grand

If you want a bigger Suzuki than a Jimny, but a Vitara is perhaps a little dated for you, then you are looking at the Grand Vitara. Also you are looking at spending more money, too.

Launched at about the same time as the Jimny, the first of the Grand Vitaras was obviously a far more expensive machine, and this is reflected in its second-hand value nowadays. Very early V6 five-doors mainly change hands for less than £7,000–£8,000, depending on whether you're buying privately or from a dealer, while an early GV1600 or GV2000 will still fetch £6,000–£7,000 depending on its mileage and condition. Look at what you're getting for your money though, compared with vehicles like the 'MkI' Toyota RAV4, and suddenly a

second-hand Grand Vitara looks like excellent value; which it can be.

It is always difficult in any book like this to quote exact price guidelines. After all, this isn't a monthly magazine that can change its values to suit sudden changes in market conditions. That is why the prices illustrated here are a general guide only, and you should always check the exact value of the vehicle you're interested in, by looking in one of the specialist price guides on sale at newsagents everywhere. These give an accurate idea of whether or not you're being asked to pay too much.

This is something that can change dramatically over a period of just a few months. At the time of writing, Suzuki has been heavily discounting brand-new Jimnys and Grand Vitaras for quite some time, with as much as 20–25 per cent 'knocked off' before you even start any serious haggling. This all sounds like great news, of

Early Grand Vitara V6 five-doors are excellent value these days, offering lots of equipment, excellent performance and that unmistakable V6 engine note, for not a great deal of money. This well looked after example from 1999 makes a tempting buy, and will be significantly cheaper than a five-door Toyota RAV4 of similar age. *(Author)*

A less predictable second-hand choice than a three-door Freelander, the Suzuki GV1600 and GV2000 models offer attractive, chunky styling and a fun driving style. Like the other Grand Vitaras, they're now within financial reach of most buyers of used 4x4s. There's very little excuse for not owning one these days! *(Author)*

course, but it is likely to have a knock-on effect on used Suzuki values over the next couple of years, and some major variations could be occurring. Serious new-car discounts traditionally mean heavier depreciation as time goes on, and there is no reason to think that Suzuki will be any different. Bear this in mind when buying any Suzuki 4x4 that is still 'in its prime'.

Warranties and dealers

A question often asked when it comes to buying a second-hand all-wheel-drive Suzuki is whether it is best to buy privately or from a dealer. And the answer is … well, it depends on the age and type of model you're interested in.

If the Suzuki you're looking at is less than three years old, for example, it is likely to still be covered its manufacturer's three-year warranty – in which case there is

relatively little risk involved in buying privately or (if you're feeling a bit more brave) even from a car auction.

Don't always assume that a warranty is still valid though, as any number of factors can make any car company's original warranty suddenly become null and void. Check, for example, that the required services have been carried out at the correct intervals by a Suzuki-franchised dealer. Similarly, check the mileage of the vehicle, as Suzuki's warranty has an upper limit of 60,000 miles; the car may well be only 18 months old and, in theory, halfway through its warranty period, but if the mileage stands at 58,000 already, then the warranty is actually on the verge of expiring. It might seem like an obvious point, but it is one worth remembering.

When buying any modern Suzuki 4x4 from a dealer, of course, it should come automatically with its own used-car warranty. This is one of the reasons why buyers are prepared to pay more money when buying from a dealer, as they assume that a degree of peace of mind is on offer, but that is not necessarily the case…

With any used car warranty, it always pays to read the small print in detail. Yes, it is almost certain to cover

major components like the engine, transmission and so on, but it won't cover 'fair wear and tear', which means you'll almost certainly be paying for your own brake pads if they're showing wear after 20,000 miles. You also need to ascertain whether the warranty covers all electrical and electronic items, as these can prove expensive if they fail. Similarly with the catalytic converter, and bear in mind too, that if you take your Suzuki off-roading and any kind of damage occurs that results in some kind of component failure, your warranty is unlikely to cover this … assuming, of course, that the reason for the failure is spotted by the garage!

The rarities

We have looked in this chapter at the kind of SJs, Vitaras, Jimnys and Grand Vitaras that are available for specific budgets, and as these are the most popular Suzuki 4x4s around, that's logical enough. But what if you fancy something a bit unusual?

Rarest of all off-road Suzukis is the LJ80, detailed in Chapter One. With fewer than 2,000 sold in the UK, as well as the model's tendency to rust at an alarming rate, it is little wonder that few survive now, but if your

Suzuki of choice just has to be an LJ80, what should you pay for such a vehicle?

This is a difficult question, if only because many of those that have survived are now highly modified and used solely for off-roading. What they're worth is entirely up to what can be agreed between the vendor and any prospective purchaser, but we certainly aren't talking more than a few hundred pounds, surely?

Not quite as rare as the LJ80 is what is undoubtedly Suzuki's oddest, most bizarre 4x4 of all time: the X-90. The only reason I haven't mentioned it up until now is because I can see little point in even considering owning one. Still, it is a Suzuki 4x4, and so, for the sake of completeness, it is included here.

The X-90, based on the Vitara chassis and running gear, was a rounded and blobby-looking two-seater with a choice of two- or four-wheel drive. Suzuki called

Above: A Suzuki specialist will have a wider choice of models available, all on one site. They'll also offer expert knowledge and useful advice to help you make the most of your 4x4. Haggle hard and they might even throw in a few extra accessories with your purchase...
(Author)

Below: Ludicrous and pointless is what most onlookers tended to think of the X-90 of the 1990s. The world just didn't need a blobby-looking two-seater 4x4. Suzuki struggled to sell this bizarre creation; no wonder it was soon dropped from most European markets.
(Suzuki GB)

it their '... radical funster'. Most of the motoring press of the 1990s called it a complete waste of time.

It is difficult to see what kind of a market Suzuki were aiming for with the X-90. As a two-seater, it was about as useful on the school run as a moped, and with the kind of styling that people laughed at rather than gazed at in admiration, it was only ever going to appeal to buyers with an obsession for self-deprecation.

The X-90 never managed more than 200–300 sales a year in the UK, and it wasn't long before the model was dropped altogether. It is not sought-after second-hand, so values tend to be low nowadays. If you like the unusual, it could just be the bargain you're looking for, but always bear in mind that, when you're fed up with it, you have to find someone else who likes X-90s and who is going to buy it from you ... and that's not going to be easy.

Part of me wants to admire Suzuki for being brave enough to launch the X-90 in Europe, and yet, I can't help thinking they were just plain daft!

X-90 with twin roof panels removed.

Get out of your box

Chapter Seven

Taking the plunge

You've made your decision about which Suzuki 4x4 you want. Or, perhaps, more simply which one you can afford. Now it's time to start going around and checking out examples that are for sale. Before you do this though, you need to know what it is you are looking for, what can go wrong, and how you can best avoid getting ripped-off.

Before we get on to the specifics, I will just offer a few words of caution about buying used cars in general. At the best of times, it is a minefield of dangers and pitfalls, and when you see a Suzuki that seems to be exactly the one you have been searching high and low for, it is all too easy to get carried away in the excitement and forget some basic procedures. That's when you are particularly vulnerable.

So, for a start, when buying any used vehicle, only ever arrange to meet the vendor at their own home or

Can you be sure the Suzuki you're buying has been serviced and maintained in accordance with the manufacturer's recommendations? Do the VIN and engine numbers tally with those shown on the V5 Registration Document? These are the kind of questions you should be asking before you buy any used car. Happily, this GV1600 is all present and correct – with a full service history, HPI check and in good order throughout. *(Author)*

(in the case of a dealer) at their premises. Meeting 'halfway' or arranging to have the car brought to your address is a classic ploy used by vendors who don't actually own the vehicles in question.

When you get to the vendor's house, ask to see the vehicle's V5 Registration Document and check that the vendor's name and the address shown on the V5 correspond with where you actually are. If you have any doubts or concerns, simply walk away. And if there's no V5 offered with the vehicle at all ('I haven't long moved house and the log book's still at DVLA', the vendor may claim), don't buy the vehicle under any circumstances, no matter how tempting the car may seem.

Checking the genuineness of a vehicle goes much further, though. Still with the V5 in your hand, take a look at the Suzuki's VIN number (usually found under the bonnet or, on later examples, on a plate on top of the dashboard which is visible through the windscreen); check it with the number printed on the V5 and, if there's any discrepancy whatsoever, don't even consider buying the car. It's that simple.

At this stage, you also need to be looking into the car's service history, to check that what the vendor claims to be a full service history actually is, as well as using this to help verify the mileage. Never accept a vendor's claim that '...the service book is still at the garage; I forgot to pick it up when I had the car serviced last week.' If a service history is boasted about, you want to be able to see it in front of you before you even consider making an offer.

Don't be afraid to spend time carefully studying the service book and any previous MoT certificates that are with the car, too. Check that all the mileages shown on certain dates tally with what's being claimed about the vehicle. You might even want to make a note of the previous owner's name and address, and contact them before you hand over any money to ensure they can back-up what you have been told, and vouch for the car's history.

Another obvious point when viewing any used car is to look for signs of a forced entry, which relates to the previous point about checking out the vendor's actual ownership. It is a sad fact of life that many thousands of cars get broken into each year, so any signs of a break-in may simply have occurred during the current keeper's ownership, so don't be afraid to ask, because there is no reason why they should hide this from you. If, however, you can clearly see that a door lock has been forced, the steering column shroud looks strangely loose or you can see signs of shattered

glass inside the car, you have every right to have your suspicions aroused when the vendor denies all knowledge.

You also need to be on the lookout for signs of previous accident damage. On younger vehicles in particular, check for mismatched paintwork (colour, finish and so on); ripples in body panels (possible evidence of body filler or poor repair work); signs of 'over-spray'; wheels that seem out of alignment, or the obvious replacement of 'inner' panel work under the bonnet. The list goes on, but just a couple of these points should be enough to make you suspicious and question the vendor's claim that '... it has never been in an accident'.

How thoroughly you follow this kind of advice will depend partly on how much you're paying for your Suzuki, how old it is and what you're intending to use it for. Let's face it, checking for panel damage on a 20-year-old SJ that's going to be used purely off-road is not going to be as important to you as it would be for the buyer of a 12-month-old Grand Vitara. Be realistic in your approach, but always be on the lookout for vendors' stories that somehow just don't 'add up'.

One final point worth mentioning before we move on to the specifics of various Suzukis is this: professional car inspections. You can pay anything between £100 and £200 for an expert to come along and thoroughly examine the vehicle you are thinking of buying. The AA and RAC carry out such inspections, as do many private companies. Obviously, when it comes to a £500 SJ, it is not an economically viable proposition; on a vehicle of such value, you can't exactly expect perfection. But I would advise anybody thinking of buying a more expensive used car to consider paying for an independent inspection. If they find any minor faults you might have missed, you will be able to use this to negotiate the price downwards; and if they discover something major that makes you think twice about buying the car, surely that's also money well spent?

Such examinations usually include an HPI (or similar) check to ensure the car in question has never been registered as stolen or previously written-off in an accident. This is essential information, and is available to anybody with a phone and a credit or debit card to pay for it. Even if you decide against a full independent inspection of a used vehicle, failure to have an HPI check carried out is arguably very foolish indeed.

With the generalities out of the way then, what kind of specifics are involved with anybody about to take the plunge into second-hand Suzuki 4x4 ownership...?

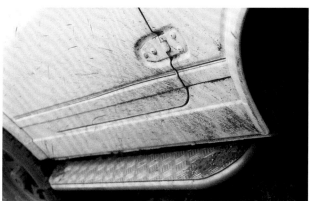

Left: An SJ's front wings are particularly prone to rusting, especially just above the front bumper. This example shows obvious signs of previous corrosion and more recent repairs with body filler. It's not pretty but it might scrape through an MoT pass. (Author)

Centre: The area that would be called a 'sill' on any other car is obviously less structural on an SJ with its separate chassis. Nevertheless, major corrosion here can result in MoT failure. Check it out before you buy. (Author)

Bottom: Are the electrics as they should be? Do all the lights work? An off-road SJ that regularly encounters deep-water wading or lashings of mud can soon find itself with electrical gremlins. (Author)

SJ, Santana and Samurai

As mentioned in Chapter Six, one of the main problems with the SJ series is its tendency to rust. While these tiny funsters are no more liable to corrosion than most other affordable vehicles launched in the early 1980s, this by no means makes them immune. Also, neglected examples that have perhaps done more than their fair share of off-roading or rough-terrain work over the years are particularly prone to corrosion.

In terms of where to look for rust on any SJ, Santana or Samurai, the simple answer is: everywhere. The good news is that the chassis on these tiddly 4x4s is pretty robust; even so, it pays to check the whole of the underside for signs of rot, poor quality welding or fresh underseal. If the underneath of an SJ has been 'patch-welded' to get it through this year's MoT, can you be sure the repair work will still be road legal next year? There are plenty of folk out there offering 'tarted-up' old bangers with next-to-no-chance of making it through another test when the time comes.

It's not just chassis rot on an SJ that can cause rust-induced MoT failure; body panels are also particularly prone. Unlike days of old when the odd hole or two in the panels of a vehicle with a strong separate chassis wouldn't have resulted in automatic MoT failure, nowadays it will. Today's MoT test places much greater emphasis on the danger to other road users and pedestrians caused by jagged, rusty holes in panels. So even though an SJ relies on its panel work for strength less than a more conventional monocoque-designed used car, it still needs to be 'in one piece'.

Just about every panel on an SJ will rust if left to its own devices. Front wings are particularly susceptible, especially at their most forward point (just above the bumper), as are all around the front wheelarches and the indicator repeater unit. Most of this is caused by a build-up of mud, road salt and general 'crud' over the

Left: Both the 970cc (shown here) and 1,298cc SJ engines are reliable and long-lived with regular maintenance. This example is generally unloved and uncared for, yet still provides its owner with reliable transport and instant starting. (Author)

Opposite: Few SJ interiors are perfect, and this one's no exception! As long as everything works though, what more can we expect from a vehicle dating back to 1982? It's important to check the state of the floor before buying, as serious corrosion isn't uncommon. (Author)

years, so if your front wings are good it's essential you clean underneath them, in all their nooks and crannies, with a jet wash or similar to ensure no future build-up occurs.

The outer 'sill' panels are also prone to rot, as are the bottoms of the doors just above them. Depending on how fussy you are about aesthetics, these can be relatively easily repaired (or even replaced, depending on how much you want to spend) as they are fairly flat in design.

The rear wheelarches can also be a rot spot as can the back of the rear arches, essentially the bottom of the rear-quarter panels, and you will be lucky if you don't find signs of bubbling, filled repairs or just a lack of solid metal. It may all need dealing with to make an SJ road legal.

On hard-top SJs, rear tailgates are also renowned for rotting along their bottom edges and around the window rubber. Then, of course, there is inside the car, where the boot floor, foot wells and general floor pan can do a remarkable impression of a sieve after a few years. Soft-top SJs are particularly vulnerable in this way, mainly because old hoods tend to leak at an alarming rate and there is often a build-up of water

trapped inside the car, particularly as the original drain holes tend to get blocked up. Drill more drain holes, get rid of the water, try to keep the floor dry and you might just be in with a chance of keeping some metal under your feet.

Because of the cheap-and-cheerful nature of the SJ series and the fact that values of early examples were rock-bottom at the end of the 1990s, many ended up being scrapped simply because they were uneconomical to repair. That was a shame, because a couple of days spent with a welding torch would have got many an MoT-failed SJ back on the road, but anybody paying a professional welder to do such work is invariably deterred by the cost of the labour involved, and understandably so. These machines are still so often seen as 'throwaway' items.

On the mechanical front, it is much better news, of course. Both the 970cc and 1,298cc 'four-pot' engines are rugged, long-lasting units that seem to take hard work in their stride. Even on examples that have covered well over 100,000 miles (which many have), the engines themselves should be showing few problems as long as they have received a modicum of basic maintenance over the years.

There is more to the mechanics than just the engine though, and SJs have their trouble spots. Carburettor wear isn't uncommon, although any symptoms of hesitation or general rough-running can often be cured with new carb jets; the difference this

makes can be quite dramatic, and it is an inexpensive repair. Even if a carburettor is dead, a second-hand or reconditioned replacement can usually be found at a realistic price.

SJ transmissions tend to get noisy with age, with a lot of 'whine' not uncommon in first and second gears. This doesn't necessarily imply imminent problems though, as gearboxes showing such symptoms have been known to go on for several more years without hassle.

When trying any SJ for the first time, it is essential you check out the dual-range transfer box. Does it change from two- to four-wheel drive without difficulty? Does the car drive backwards and forwards in four-wheel drive, in *both* low and high ratio modes? Are there any untoward noises that might spell problems when you're in four-wheel drive? Not every SJ owner is particularly caring, and some have been known to force their vehicles into four-wheel drive before they are at a complete standstill. On a modern Jimny this isn't a problem, but with an SJ it can cause damage and wear. Make sure you're confident that all is working as it should be before you decide on buying the vehicle.

Checking over an SJ is, in most other respects, pretty much like examining any other type of old car. You need to ensure crucial safety items are all as they should be: do the brakes pull up squarely; do the dampers still have plenty of life left in them; are the leaf springs in good order; do the tyres have enough tread to legally last a while longer; is the steering reasonably precise?

Don't be afraid to climb into a pair of overalls and crawl underneath an SJ either, checking for leaks (from the steering box, shock absorbers, engine, transmission…), any splits in rubber joints or sleeves, any corrosion you might have missed, signs of anything 'dropping off', the state of the exhaust, and so on. The ground clearance on an SJ is sufficient to enable you to carry out some checks without the car jacked up – but *always* make sure the vehicle hasn't been run within the last hour, or you could end up burning yourself on the exhaust.

The vendor may not object to you jacking up the car and taking a really good look at the underside, but *always* remember though, *never* to crawl underneath a car that is supported solely by a jack. If you can't support it on a set of axle stands, forget the idea.

Above: The SJ's tailgate (on a hard-top) and the rear door (on a soft-top) can be prone to rust. Fortunately, this one is in fine condition and won't need any attention for quite some time. *(Author)*

Below: This 1994 Vitara Verdi is in impressive condition, but not all of them are as smart. Cosmetics have a big part to play when valuing any Vitara, as many examples are still bought for their head-turning looks. As you can see, this one is sporting more than a few accessories, including a chrome A-bar and side steps, plus wider wheels and tyres. *(Author)*

Vitara spotting

Many of the checks that you would carry out when buying any model from the SJ series apply equally to the Vitara, as the two vehicles aren't dissimilar in basic layout. The best news though, is that the Vitara isn't as rust-prone as the SJ, which makes finding a good example, arguably, less of an arduous task.

That said, elderly Vitaras do still rust, but (so far) this tends to be less 'life threatening' in terms of MoT failure than with an SJ. And, of course, how much cosmetic corrosion may concern you depends on what you're going to use your Vitara for, and how much you will be paying for it.

Any Vitara under £2,000 is likely to be showing the early stages of some kind of corrosion, although not necessarily to a drastic extent. Cosmetically, the edges of the wheelarches can start to bubble, which doesn't look too bad while the paint on top is still present. Always be aware though, that where there are paint bubbles, there is some sort of corrosion that is working its way through from beneath, and this will only get worse. Similarly, the bottoms of the

Above: From the sublime to the ridiculous! What was once a basic long-wheelbase Vitara is now a Ford Cosworth-engined super-4x4 complete with drastically lowered suspension, amazing paint job and an all-new interior. The trouble is, how do you value a Vitara like this? Whatever it's worth, it's an amazing creation, courtesy of the enthusiasts at Suzi Q's. *(Author)*

Left: Check out the bonnet of the Vitara you're interested in. Are there any dents or 'dings'? They do seem particularly prone to these. *(Author)*

Below: A Vitara hood that's showing the classic signs of age and wear: it's dirty, it's worn and the zips look well past their best. Use this as a bargaining tool though, as a full replacement hood may not cost as much as you think – and will absolutely transform the appearance of your Vitara. *(Author)*

A Vitara Verdi gets treated to a complete new hood at Suzi Q's. This specialist company has its own-spec new hoods made to order, and they're claimed to be of superior quality to the originals. The tinted side and rear 'windows' are a neat touch. *(Author)*

doors on Vitaras can suffer, as can the bottom edge of the tailgate.

Vitara bonnets seem very prone to minor dents and 'dings' where they've been slammed shut over the years; while water penetration around the windscreen rubber can lead to creeping rust, again causing the paint bubbling effect mentioned earlier.

Structurally though, it is pretty good news. It is fairly rare for a Vitara to need major repairs to its steel chassis, and the whole of the underside (floor pans, footwells, boot floor and so on) seems better protected and less susceptible to rot than the SJ's.

A major factor when buying a soft-top Vitara will be the condition of its hood, as these become tatty with age and generally wear out, especially if they have been removed a lot over the years. White hoods, in particular, can look dreadful when dirty or torn. In a way though, you can use this to your advantage, and the first step is to price up the cost of having a brand-new hood fitted via a specialist such as Suzi Q's. In my experience, you will find this is actually less expensive than you might fear. Poor hood condition can be used to negotiate the price of a Vitara downwards, safe in

the knowledge that the 'discount' you achieve will more than cover the cost of a new hood. There is nothing like a brand-new hood for transforming the look of any soft-top Vitara, while there is nothing like a worn, ripped or dirty old hood for bringing an asking price down.

Bear in mind, too, that a tatty old hood can mean condensation and plenty of leaks inside any soft-top Vitara that is getting on in years. Condensation can and will occur in any example that tends to sit outside for long periods, and this in turn can cause mould and dampness on all the fabrics – from the upholstery to the seat belts, and to the inside of the hood itself. Not only is this unpleasant for those on board, it also means rapid deterioration of the interior. Always bear this in mind when viewing what seems to be a clean and pristine interior on a hot summer's day; what will it be like next winter?

An area of cosmetics you should also pay careful attention to is that of modifications. Large numbers of Vitaras can still be found with massively flared wheelarches, side skirts, fat alloys and the like. Always ensure though, that such changes have been carried out well and to a professional standard. Are the bulging add-on arches properly fitted and is their paintwork of good quality? Have they acquired a few 'parking grazes' because of their sheer width? Have the side skirts cracked where people have perhaps stood on them, or where they have caught on a kerb? Are the aftermarket alloy wheels still shiny, free of scrapes and corrosion? If possible, always ascertain where the modifications were carried out and how much they cost; this will help to sort the DIY messes from the professional high-quality jobs.

With Vitaras getting increasingly cheaper and therefore appealing to larger numbers of off-roaders than ever before, you need to make sure the one you are viewing isn't suffering from any 'rough stuff' damage. Look carefully underneath for evidence: check, for example, whether the sump is dented; if there are signs of scrapes on the exhaust or the floor

Above, left: Any Vitara Soft Top can suffer from condensation and damp inside, which can play havoc with the upholstery, seat belts and carpets eventually. This example's interior is in excellent order, mainly due to two replacement hoods during its lifetime ... so far. *(Author)*

Above, top: If the Vitara you're looking at has had a few mods carried out, like these add-on flared wheelarches, can you be sure the work has been done properly? Don't be afraid to ask the vendor lots of questions to satisfy your curiosity. Check, too, that wheelarches like these aren't suffering from scrapes and scratches due to their extreme width. *(Author)*

Above: Expensive-looking alloys can transform the appearance of any Vitara, but don't fall into the trap of paying over the odds for any example that already has them fitted. Vendors can't realistically expect to recoup the full cost of such mods when they come to sell their vehicles. *(Author)*

pan; is there a whole quarry's worth of mud caked to the underside; are the front struts bent (in extreme cases); do the steering and brakes feel as they should; and does the dual-range transfer box work as Suzuki intended, in all the gears and in both ratios?

Above: Are you sure the mileage on the Vitara you're inspecting is correct? Does the condition of the interior support this? Have you checked the service history for proof? You can't be too careful when buying. *(Author)*

Below: If you're buying from a dealer, don't be afraid to ask to inspect the Vitara on a ramp so you can get a clear idea of the condition of the underside. If buying privately, it still pays to crawl underneath, but only if the vehicle is supported on axle stands. Never rely on a jack alone! *(Author)*

Look for other clues too, such as whether all-terrain tyres are fitted; this would suggest a reasonable amount of off-road work at some point. Is there perhaps even an engine snorkel installed, as this is obvious proof of off-road modifications. If you intend to use your cheap-and-cheerful Vitara primarily off-road yourself, such mods can be a positive advantage, but if what you're after is, first and foremost, a road car for everyday use, you would be better off looking for an example that hasn't experienced life in the mud so far.

In other aspects, buying a Vitara is pretty much like buying any other second-hand car. Carry out all the usual checks and, chances are, you won't go far wrong. Fortunately, all the Vitara power plants (1.6 petrol, 2.0 diesel, 2.0 V6) are reliable and long-lived, being generally capable of very high mileages before major repair work is required. Carburettor wear on early examples isn't uncommon as the miles mount, so if a fuel-injected model is within financial reach you could find this a better long-term proposition. As ever though, much depends on the level of maintenance that has been carried out in the past, and you should always satisfy yourself that the correct servicing and repair work has been done over the years. If there are any doubts, walk away and look for another Vitara; there are plenty of them about to choose from.

An area that is always worth investigating thoroughly is the Vitara's electrics. Although the electrical and electronic components themselves all seem reliable in long-term use, these are often some of the first things to suffer at the hands of regular off-roading. Does everything electrical work OK? Double-check just to make sure, and bear in mind that deep water wading and seriously muddy off-roading can play havoc with lights, wiring, alternators and the like.

One final word of warning about buying a used Vitara concerns special editions, with the 1994 Verdi models being a good example. Marketed as a 'limited edition', but hardly rare by any standards, the metallic green soft-top Vitara Verdi offered a few eye-catching goodies (smarter interior, white hood and so on) over the standard model. But is it worth paying any extra for one on the used market, all these years on? I'd say it probably isn't, but it depends how badly you want one. Just make sure you are not swayed by a persuasive vendor who claims the 'limited editions' are worth twice as much as an ordinary Vitara ... they're not.

Time for a final check ... so make sure the lights are working and there's plenty of tread on the spare tyre that's lurking under that canvas cover. It's so easy to forget such essentials when giving any car the once-over. *(Author)*

Equally, don't assume you have to pay somebody what they have spent on modifications and add-ons when you're buying their Vitara. Just because somebody's forked out £3,000 on decent alloys, matching tyres, lots of chrome and maybe even a smart new paint job doesn't mean the vehicle is worth £3,000 more on the second-hand market. In fact, if you haggle

Has the Jimny or Grand Vitara you're interested in been used much off-road? Look for damage and check out what the owner says about its previous useage. Are they telling the truth...? *(Author)*

hard, you will find buying a well-modified Vitara could save you quite a lot of money compared with having the work done yourself on a standard example; just a thought.

Jimny and Grand Vitara

Launched in 1998, both the Jimny and Grand Vitara ranges are the 'babies' of the Suzuki 4x4 line-up. Combine their relative youth (well, compared with a Suzuki SJ anyway) with the fact that they make more use of galvanised steel in their construction than any Suzuki before them, and you have a convincing argument for finding a bit extra cash and opting for one of these instead of a Vitara. Equally, anybody in the market for a Land Rover Freelander or a used Toyota RAV4 should find a Grand Vitara a much better value offering instead.

Suzuki's reputation for reliability, longevity and durability is well deserved, and both the Jimny and the Grand Vitara continue this fine tradition. Even the Spanish-built Jimny Soft Top and the Canadian-built GV

Soft Top seem to offer near-Japanese levels of build quality, and neither of them seems to suffer any more mechanical woes or reliability problems than the rest of the range. All of which is excellent news for today's potential buyers.

Like any vehicles that date back to the late-1990s though, problems can arise as time goes by – although in this case they tend to occur mainly due to very high mileage, total neglect, or poor maintenance. The main lesson here is to apply a healthy dose of common sense when buying a used Jimny or Grand Vitara, and only buy the best and/or youngest example you can afford.

For a start, forget any vehicle that doesn't come with a full service history. Even the very earliest examples were still covered by their manufacturer's new-car warranty as (relatively) recently as the

WHAT THE PRESS SAID – Jimny Soft Top

'Forget hairdressers; this Suzuki is built to lap up tricky terrain and should prove reliable. But the fun stops when you try to take the hood off, open the rear tailgate or coax power out of the engine.' (*4x4*, November 2002)

Above: The engines used in Jimnys and Grand Vitaras cover quite a wide range of petrol and diesel powerplants. Without exception though, they're reliable, dependable and capable of covering high mileages with ease. Shown here is the smooth and powerful 2.5-litre V6. *(Author)*

Left: Look for damage to the Jimny's and Grand Vitara's large plastic bumpers. They're prone to knocks during the school run and the urban grind they're usually forced to endure. *(Author)*

end of 2001, so if there is a lack of service records or paperwork in general you have every right to be suspicious.

Once a vehicle is out of its initial warranty period, it is not unusual for it to be serviced and maintained away from the official Suzuki dealer network. This in itself need not be a problem, but any garage should still be expected to keep the Suzuki's service book stamped and up to date. So, if there are a few scheduled services that appear to have been missed ... well, alarm bells should start ringing in your head.

Both of the Jimny's 1.3-litre powerplants are reliable and durable in everyday use, but do bear in mind that, due to their small capacity and 'buzzy' nature, they tend to get worked hard. I have heard 50,000-mile Jimnys

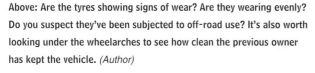

Above: Are the tyres showing signs of wear? Are they wearing evenly? Do you suspect they've been subjected to off-road use? It's also worth looking under the wheelarches to see how clean the previous owner has kept the vehicle. (Author)

Top, right: Introduced in 1998, both the Jimny and Grand Vitara are relatively young models by Suzuki standards. There should be no reason, therefore, to buy one without a full service history and a warranted mileage. (Author)

Bottom, right: Grand Vitara interiors can suffer, as these are favourite 'school run' cars and family vehicles. It's amazing how a hoard of destructive children can damage a 4x4's interior! Happily, this example – even in the luggage area – is immaculate throughout. (Author)

that sound a bit 'rattly' at tickover and when pushed to the limit, though they seem to be in a reasonable state of health still with as much power as they ever did. These were never refined vehicles compared with their upmarket 'supermini' rivals, so don't be too surprised by what you hear.

The bigger Grand Vitara's engines, by definition, need to work less hard to provide adequate performance … and it shows. Even the GV1600's four-cylinder engine is relatively smooth and seems trouble-free even on high-mileage examples; likewise the 2.0-litre. The turbo-diesel Grand Vitara isn't the quietest or most refined 'oil-burner' around, but it is a superbly reliable engine and seems to take high mileage and hard work in its stride. As for the V6 … well, this is an absolute delight and, again, is a fantastically reliable unit.

If all this is starting to sound rather boring, I make no apologies. If I were writing about 1.8-litre K-Series-engined Land Rover Freelanders, I could wax lyrical about their reputation for head gasket failure, their build quality issues and the electrical woes on early examples. But I'm not; I'm writing about Suzuki Jimnys and Grand Vitaras, and frankly, there's hardly any bad news to talk about.

What there is tends to be caused by disrespectful owners. Interiors can become tatty on examples that have been filled with destructive young children every day of their lives. The large plastic bumpers tend to suffer undue damage thanks to the bad parking habits of forever-in-a-hurry parents on the school run. And ... and ... there's not much else.

One thing worth mentioning here is that a fair proportion of Grand Vitaras (and even some Jimnys) are ordered brand-new with automatic transmission. Happily, if this is something that appeals to you on the used market, you have very little to worry about, as the auto 'boxes tend to be as long-lived and reliable as the five-speed manual set-ups. Indeed, the Grand Vitara V6 with automatic transmission is a fantastic combination, making for an effortless on-road driving style. Just make sure you're satisfied with the auto gearbox itself, (ie does it change up and down the gears as it should, particularly on steep hills), and does the 'kick down' facility work quickly and effectively when you press sharply on the accelerator? Hopefully there are likely to be few problems.

Jimnys and Grand Vitaras are often seen as durable workhorses and so rarely need cleaning and hardly ever need attention under the bonnet. This is all well and good, but it means they are rarely cherished by adoring owners. Bear this in mind when buying, and always be on the lookout for signs of neglect. Buy one that has not been crashed, but

A fair proportion of Grand Vitaras now available second-hand are fitted with automatic transmission. Is this something you really want? If so, the gearbox itself should give little cause for concern. In V6 guise in particular, an automatic Grand Vitara is a joy to drive. (Author)

has been serviced at the correct intervals, that's not been abused off-road and that hopefully, has a realistic mileage in its favour and you can't go far wrong. These are by no means the most expensive 4x4s on the market, but they are amongst the most reliable, a fact that has been confirmed by countless consumer and owner satisfaction surveys over the years.

Chapter **Eight**

Running your Suzuki

Few Suzuki 4x4s could ever be criticised for being expensive to run. In fact, that would be something of an alien concept to a company so famed for its compact cars. Suzuki is a manufacturer of affordable vehicles and, as such, always needs to ensure they remain competitive in terms of their running costs.

What does this really equate to in the real world though? Buyers of brand-new Suzukis in the USA are somewhat spoiled in this respect, as the company's American website enables potential buyers to make direct comparisons between a Suzuki product and any of its major rivals. And what an informative and useful facility this is. We put it to the test by comparing a new entry-level Grand Vitara V6 (known simply as the Vitara in the States) with an equivalent five-door Toyota RAV4, and within a few seconds we had all the direct comparisons and figures on screen.

In 2004, the Suzuki was roughly $1,700 cheaper than the Toyota, although the RAV4 had the edge on economy with an official 'City' figure of 24mpg compared with the Vitara's 19mpg. The information given covered both cars' technical specifications, engines (2.5-litre V6 for the Suzuki; 2.4-litre four-cylinder for the Toyota), equipment levels (no electric sunroof on the Vitara; standard fitment on the RAV4) and a whole lot more. The website is fun to use, is amazingly useful for buyers in the States, and it gives choosing an American-spec 4x4 a whole new dimension.

Sadly though, there are different rules and regulations regarding the sale and marketing of new cars in Europe. This means, for example, that Suzuki GB's website is unable to offer comparative information on rival products, even if the importers wanted to. The solution, of course, is for potential buyers to plough through magazines and brochures themselves to gain all the information and comparisons they need, although this is obviously a time-consuming business. Hopefully then, the facts and figures given in this chapter will save some of that hard work.

New-car value?

There's never been any argument with Suzuki over the pricing of their 4x4s. From 1978 to the present day, just about every all-wheel-drive Suzuki has managed to significantly undercut its major rivals on price. Nowadays, you only have to look at the current cost of a new Jimny, Grand Vitara or XL-7 to realise this.

The Grand Vitara in particular tends to cost much less to buy than its main competitors, with the Land Rover Freelander, Toyota RAV4 and Honda CR-V all being priced significantly higher when compared like-for-like. The fact that models such as the Grand Vitara also come extremely well equipped is the icing on the cake for many Suzuki buyers.

But there's more to a value-for-money list price than that; to achieve real value, a vehicle also needs to offer healthy long-term residuals. This is an area that is of particular interest to Suzuki, as the company embarks upon some major discounts and special offers from time to time, a move that traditionally tends to adversely affect residual values. In Suzuki's case though, this doesn't seem to have happened to any great extent.

Opposite: It's much easier for buyers in the States to make direct comparisons between any Suzuki and its main rivals, as all the information you need is carried on the company's excellent American website – from prices and technical details to equipment levels and performance figures. Sadly, Suzuki's European websites don't provide the same depth of information. *(Suzuki GB)*

By the time the last of the Vitaras had arrived in the shape of the 4u and 4u² special editions, the model's residuals weren't as strong as they once were. By 2000, the Vitara was no longer the trendiest thing on the road; as a result, *What Car?* was predicting 65 per cent depreciation over three years and 36,000 miles. *(Suzuki GB)*

Suzuki 4x4s have always held their value reasonably well. Back in 2000, Britain's *What Car?* magazine was offering some interesting information on the then-current range of Suzukis in terms of their retained value after three years and 36,000 miles. Top of the pile came the Grand Vitara 2.0 TD and the GV2000, each said to retain 40 per cent of their list prices; the then ageing Vitara range suffered more, retaining just 35 per cent. This compared with comparative residuals of around 48 per cent for most Land Rover Freelanders, 39 per cent for a Mitsubishi Shogun Pinin 1.8 GLS and an astonishing 54 per cent for a Honda CR-V 2.0 LS.

Bringing things slightly more up to date, *Auto Express* magazine came up with some interesting figures in 2004, again comparing the residuals of various models after three years of average miles. Interestingly, they pitched the Grand Vitara 2.0 TD at a retained value of 43 per cent of its list price, with the Jimny coming in at

40–43 per cent, depending on the exact model. These in themselves are reasonably healthy figures, but when you add into the equation that most buyers of such vehicles at that time probably achieved discounts of 15–20 per cent, suddenly the residual forecasts look rather impressive.

Interestingly, *Auto Express* was claiming comparative residuals of 47–49 per cent for the Land Rover

WHAT THE PRESS SAID – Running an SJ410

'To date, this little Suzuki hasn't needed anything spending in terms of running costs – apart from petrol, of course. I haven't even had to top up her oil level, so sound is this engine. Or so it seems. I will, though, be carrying out some investigative work soon, if only to try to cure the slightly annoying flat spot when pulling away from standstill. Will more problems be unearthed along the way? Will C438 RFE really be able to offer me reliability throughout the winter and beyond? Whatever, I'm content in the knowledge that 4x4 bargains ARE out there, and even the most impoverished of today's motorists can choose to go the off-road route. It's true.' *(4x4 Mart, February 2003)*

Grand Vitaras tend to lose a bigger proportion of their value during the first three years than, say, a Toyota RAV4 or Honda CR-V. This is probably an unfair comparison though, as the Grand Vitara tends to get discounted much more when new than either of those two major rivals – which means you're paying a lot less for the vehicle in the first place. Shown here putting an early Grand Vitara through its paces is motoring journalist Richard Aucock. *(Author)*

A 2000-model Suzuki GV2000 held its value better than a Vitara of the same year, it seems. This was no doubt due to the fact that both the Grand Vitara and GV models were still relatively new, which meant fewer second-hand examples being available in the early years. *(Author)*

Freelander 1.8 E; 45 per cent for the Mitsubishi Shogun Pinin 1.8 Equippe, and an incredible 60 per cent for both the Honda CR-V SE Executive and the Toyota RAV4 XT2. Bear in mind though, that models like the RAV4 and the CR-V tend to get discounted less when new, so you're paying far more for the 'privilege' of owning one in the first place.

Of course, none of this is of any great concern if you're buying a well-used Suzuki that's getting on in years. Then you will tend to be more interested in the more 'everyday' running costs …

Economy drive

A question that is often asked by people considering buying a 4x4 for the first time is: How economical will it be? Inevitably, most 4x4s tend to use more fuel than similar-size 'normal' cars sharing not dissimilar powerplants. In the case of 4x4s with permanent all-wheel drive (which obviously doesn't apply to Suzuki), this is often caused by the 'driveline drag' which is par for the course when all four wheels are driven; and in the case of most Suzukis, it is down to areas like overall weight and aerodynamics.

That is why the owner of a humble Suzuki Jimny 1.3 will be reasonably content with 38–40mpg overall, when driven carefully. Meanwhile, somebody driving a 1.2 or 1.3-litre 'supermini' like a Volkswagen Lupo, Vauxhall Corsa or Ford Ka will expect more in the region of 45mpg. Suzukis are no different from other 4x4s in this respect, and an increase in fuel consumption is a fact of life for most first-time buyers of just about any SUV or off-roader.

The area of fuel economy obviously plays a big part in the overall running costs of any vehicle, as does the area of depreciation mentioned earlier. Then there are servicing costs to take into account, as well as insurance groupings, the cost of a tax disc and so on. Rather usefully, motoring magazines do much of the homework, coming up with their own 'Pence-per-mile' running costs for every new car on sale, and it really does make fascinating reading.

Worried about fuel consumption? Some canny Vitara owners have had their vehicles converted to LPG, which in the UK means almost half-price fuel compared with the cost of unleaded petrol. Unless you cover a fairly high annual mileage or you intend keeping your Vitara for a few more years though, the cost of the conversion itself might out-weigh any major advantages. Much depends on your own personal needs, your driving style and how many miles you cover per annum. (Author)

In 2004, *Auto Express* claimed a Jimny 1.3 Hard Top cost 39p per mile to run, compared with 36p per mile for the similarly priced Daihatsu Terios 1.3 Tracker. Contrasting these figures with what is claimed for 'superminis' of similar value, they quoted 36p per mile for the Skoda Fabia 1.4 Comfort; 35p per mile for the Renault Clio 1.4 Dynamique; 38p per mile for a Ford Fiesta 1.4 LX, and 34p per mile for a Honda Jazz 1.4 SE. It's an interesting consideration that, despite the poor aerodynamics and higher insurance groupings of most 4x4s, it apparently costs just one pence more per mile to run a Suzuki Jimny than a Ford Fiesta of similar price. Suddenly the argument for driving a 'normal' car looks even more precarious.

Older bargains

The older the Suzuki (or any other 4x4) you're buying, the less you will need to worry about areas like residuals and depreciation. That's because something like an early Vitara or late-model Samurai has already lost a vast proportion of its new cost, and it is unlikely to fall in value that much further. Let's face it, if you're spending £1,000 on an old 4x4, the most money you can possibly lose is, well, a few hundred quid. That's obvious.

Other concerns do arise though. How reliable will my old 4x4 be? How expensive will spare parts be? Will it become less economical with age? Will I still be able to get all the bits I need? These are all valid questions.

Happily, in the case of most Suzuki 4x4s, the answers are all very positive. For a start, the vehicles themselves are, by their very nature, extremely reliable and durable. So as long as you continue to maintain and service yours as and when required, there should be relatively few hassles ahead. Servicing costs aren't extortionate either, thanks to realistically priced spare parts in most cases, as well as the mechanical simplicity that is part of the appeal of these vehicles.

WHAT THE PRESS SAID – Running a Jimny

'Don't expect much refinement. The short wheelbase and stiffish suspension result in a quite bumpy ride quality, while the 1300cc engine, in spite of being a modern and efficient multivalve unit, needs to be revved hard to give the Jimny anything like lively performance.' (*4x4, Used 4x4 of the Year 2003*)

Above, left: At the 'banger' end of the market, concerns such as depreciation just don't matter. How can an SJ of this age depreciate much further, after all? Of far more interest to the owners of such vehicles is the cost and availability of spare parts. Happily, models like the SJ are well catered for when it comes to both new and second-hand parts and accessories. *(Author)*

Above: If you're a keen off-roader, you'll find a Vitara's running costs are as reasonable as just about any comparable 4x4. Early examples are now cheap to buy; the 1.6-litre engines are reliable, robust and fairly economical, and even the replacement of any damaged or worn parts caused by serious off-road use won't break the bank. *(Author)*

Above: Using a 'classic' Vitara every day is an economically viable proposition, particularly now that values are at sensible levels. It's still possible to pick up an immaculate, low-mileage, basic Vitara for the price of a very ordinary, very boring second-hand saloon. And in just about every respect, the Suzuki will be as cheap to run, as well as a lot more fun! *(Author)*

Below: For the ultimate in Vitara economy, the 2.0-litre diesel model is still a very popular used buy. It will take vast mileages with ease, and will provide greatly enhanced fuel economy into the bargain. This was Suzuki's first diesel 4x4 for the European market, and is highly respected by Vitara fanatics. *(Suzuki GB)*

Above: There's no shortage of Suzuki and 4x4 specialists able to offer keenly priced parts and accessories, as well as all the expertise and advice you may need. Many such companies also buy in vehicles for breaking, enabling you to pick up second-hand parts at a fraction of their new cost. *(Author)*

Above, right: Apart from a Suzuki's dual-range transfer box, there is little else about its mechanical layout that will be unfamiliar to the average DIY mechanic. The transfer boxes themselves are relatively straightforward and very reliable in long-term use, as long as they haven't been horrendously abused over the years. *(Frank Westworth)*

Right: If you're concerned about fuel economy, this is most certainly not the Grand Vitara to go for, no matter how cheap a second-hand example might seem at first glance. There's nothing wrong with the engine itself; it's gloriously smooth and powerful, but used every day in urban conditions, you'll find it's far from frugal. A Grand Vitara V6 will also prove more expensive to insure and service. *(Author)*

Apart from the slight complication of having a dual-range transfer box (which is actually a remarkably straightforward piece of kit), there's nothing about working on a Suzuki 4x4 that will be unfamiliar to any DIY mechanic who is used to working on 'normal' cars. It is all very familiar stuff and it's as uncomplicated as you're likely to find anywhere these days.

Another advantage is that because Suzuki tends to keep its vehicles in production far longer than most manufacturers, spare parts also tend to remain available a lot longer. The only real exception to this is the early LJ80, for which your local Suzuki dealer is unlikely to be able to order, say, brand-new body panels. But for the rest of the range, from the earliest SJs onwards, there's really very little that you can't buy 'off the shelf'.

Due to the popularity of all-wheel-drive Suzukis, you don't even need to stick with the manufacturer's official dealer network when it comes to obtaining parts or having your vehicle worked on. There are plenty of 4x4 specialists around (not all of them dealing solely in

Just about any original-shape Vitara will prove a practical proposition as an everyday vehicle. If the boot space is sometimes a bit small for your needs, drop down either half or all of the split/fold back seat and you'll find a large, flat load area suddenly at your disposal. (Frank Westworth)

Suzukis, but most of them with some knowledge of the marque) who will happily service, repair or modify your vehicle. There are other companies dealing in Suzuki spares, able to supply parts and accessories at prices that are lower than those of any official Suzuki dealer. Also, there's no shortage of 4x4 breakers which are ideal if you're working to a tight budget and are willing to consider fitting second-hand parts to keep costs down. Details of such companies and specialists can be found in Appendix A of this book.

One final point worth mentioning to any 4x4 first-timer is the cost of tyres, as these can sometimes be more expensive than you'd expect to pay for a 'normal' car. Even so, there are increasing numbers of budget brands now offering tyres for specific 4x4s and off-

The Grand Vitara may have lacked some of the ride quality and all-round refinement of its rivals from Toyota and Honda, but few people could knock the model's sheer value for money – both new and second-hand. *(Author)*

roaders, so the situation has greatly improved over the last few years. Much depends, of course, on the type of tyres you're going to need for your style of driving. If that means lots of off-roading for your particular Suzuki, then a set of more expensive all-terrain rubber is really the only answer.

Prove it to yourself

Of course, the only real way to prove to yourself beyond all doubt that running an all-wheel-drive Suzuki really can be an enjoyable and financially painless experience, is to go out and buy with your own hard-earned cash, whichever model takes your fancy. Just make sure though, that you apply the same level of common sense to choosing the ideal model as you hopefully will do finding the best example for your money.

Don't, for example, opt for a bargain-priced Grand Vitara 2.5 V6 if fuel economy is one of your major requirements; unlike most other Suzuki powerplants, that super-smooth V6 could never be called frugal. Similarly, if you're under 21, have a string of speeding convictions to your name, and you live in an inner city battle zone, you may find a Grand Vitara's 'Group 12' insurance rating a tad on the high side. Do a bit of homework before you make your decision and there'll obviously be less chance of you making the wrong choice.

WHAT THE PRESS SAID – Running a Grand Vitara

'For: Three-year Suzuki warranty; chunky looks; easy to drive; V6 engine powerful and refined. Against: Poor ride; not as composed as the Freelander. Best Buy: Grand Vitara V6.' *(What Car?, November 2000)*

Chapter Nine

Modifications and upgrades

Part of the main appeal of just about any Suzuki 4x4 for many owners is the ease with which it can be modified, personalised or upgraded without spending an absolute fortune in the process. That means, whether you're considering modifications to transform your Suzuki into a head-turning 'cruiser' or a wild off-road machine, you can create something unique, but still very affordable.

Much depends, of course, on just how far you want to go with both the upgrades and the expense. But with a realistic attitude, a keen eye on your priorities and a fixed target in terms of what you're trying to achieve, it's possible to get something rather special parked on your driveway that falls well within budget.

What exactly are you trying to achieve, though? Remember, after all, that the kind of modifications that are popular with owners who want to drive something unique on the road will not be suitable if you're intent on becoming a weekend off-roader. Chrome side steps, flash alloys and elaborate bull bars may look great on the street; but the first time you get stuck in a rut,

If you're thinking of modifying your Suzuki for head-turning road use, there's a plethora of add-ons and accessories waiting for you via the many 4x4 and Suzuki specialists. Of course, not everyone will want a bright pink soft-top Vitara with 'fat' alloys and massive wheelarches... *(Author)*

First stop for Jimny or Grand Vitara accessories could be your nearest Suzuki dealer. There's no shortage of choice in Suzuki's official Accessories catalogue, as this Jimny **Soft Top** proudly demonstrates. Side skirts, special alloys, silver-painted bull bar and silver headlamp surrounds create a very distinctive first impression. *(Author)*

you're knee-high in mud and slurry or you need towing out of a particularly treacherous off-road situation, you will regret your choices when you see how damaged they are. The moral of the story? Be clear what you want from your Suzuki 4x4: is it an on-road car that needs to look good at a local cruise, or is it an off-road workhorse? It's 'make your mind up' time, because your shopping list will vary hugely depending on your answer.

Neat on the street

Transforming your Suzuki into a one-off, personalised vehicle that stands out in any crowd isn't necessarily a difficult process. Vitaras are still very popular with such enthusiasts, which explains why there's such a vast array of extras, add-ons and accessories available for the model. A good proportion of Jimny owners also like to make their vehicles more individual looking, whilst

Grand Vitara fanatics are now gaining ground when it comes to this kind of expense. People with SJs and Samurais tend to use their Suzukis increasingly off-road nowadays, so this section of the chapter applies less to these models.

If it's a Jimny or a Grand Vitara that graces your driveway, it's a good idea to get a copy of Suzuki's latest Accessories catalogue for your particular model. You might be surprised by the wide range of official Suzuki accessories and merchandise available, so it's certainly well worth a look.

At the time of writing, Suzuki GB offers an impressive range of stuff for the Jimny in particular, with an upper rear spoiler (for the Hard Top), a choice of spare wheel covers, side wind deflectors, 15-inch Kalahari five-spoke alloy wheels, fog lamps and a smart-looking bull bar set-up which is especially popular. In no time at all, your Suzuki dealer will be able to supply (and fit, if you so wish) all these items and more. The end result is certainly more eye-catching than a completely standard Jimny.

Grand Vitara owners needn't feel left out; in fact, their vehicles are just as well catered for. Suzuki's current range of official accessories includes many similar

A smart, basic Vitara like this makes an excellent 'blank canvas' for any potential owner who wants to create something totally individual.

features to the Jimny line-up, albeit with the addition of 16-inch, six-spoke Gobi alloys, a removable hard-top (for the Soft Top … if you see what I mean), a wood-effect dashboard panel, a choice of four hard spare wheel cover designs, a centre arm rest, a highly useful roof rack and a detachable tow bar. Again, pick up the current catalogue from your Suzuki dealer for the latest range and up-to-date prices.

Away from official Suzuki items the choice is even wider, of course. In fact, there's an astonishing range of goodies on sale for Vitaras, Jimnys and Grand Vitaras, with Midlands-based specialists Suzi Q's being amongst the biggest suppliers. This very enthusiastic company specialises in Vitaras, but also supplies parts and accessories for other Suzuki 4x4s, as well as offering used car sales, MoT and servicing facilities, a full body shop and a same-day fitting service for any accessories or modifications purchased through themselves.

Founded in the early 1990s, Suzi Q's has become one of the biggest names in Suzuki specialists, and many of the accessories they stock are actually made specifically for them. Their chrome bull bars, side steps and kick plates for the sills are all manufactured to

their own design, with the smart company logo forming an integral part. Their range of aftermarket soft-tops too, is commissioned by themselves and feature some useful upgrades over the Suzuki originals – including tinted colour screens, extra interior lining and so on.

For those who want a 'complete package' of Vitara improvements, Suzi Q's have a range of custom packs available, the most popular one incorporating 10-inch 'Fat Boy' wheels and tyres, big wheelarches, a pair of side steps, a large front A-bar and a smart stainless-steel spare wheel cover. Buying the whole package saves a fair sum of money over ordering the items individually.

Back in 2003, *4x4 Mart* magazine chose Suzi Q's to supply them with a modified Vitara to give away as first prize in a competition. They eventually chose a 1994 Vitara Verdi (a limited edition of just 500 examples sold in the UK), and then embarked upon a series of aesthetic improvements to really make it stand out from

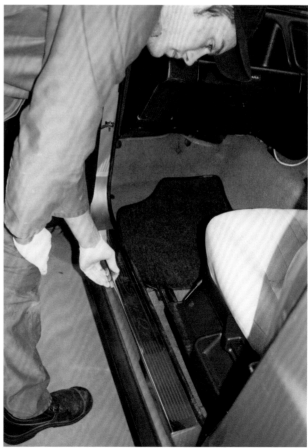

Opposite, top: The experts at Suzi Q's get cracking on another round of modifications. A smart-looking chrome bull bar (one of Suzi Q's own designs) is fitted first to this 1994 Vitara Verdi. *(Author)*

Opposite, bottom: This is how the bull bar looks once fitted; very smart indeed. The subtle Suzi Q's cut-out logo is a neat finishing touch. *(Author)*

Above: Next comes a set of chrome side steps. These are purely for decorative purposes, and are actually something of a hindrance if you intend embarking on some serious off-roading in your Vitara. For road-going examples though, they add an extra touch of style. *(Author)*

Right: A simple but effective upgrade is a pair of stainless-steel kick plates for the top of the sills. Again adorned with the Suzi Q's logo, they're a popular and inexpensive choice for many Vitara fanatics. *(Author)*

Right: If you're replacing a torn or tatty hood on an old Vitara, why not upgrade it at the same time? Standard items are readily available from Suzuki specialists and hood manufacturers; this example, designed specifically for Suzi Q's, features top-quality fabrics, tinted screens and a luxury lining. *(Author)*

Below: The finished article! What was previously a neat but very ordinary-looking Vitara Verdi was transformed in just half a day into this eye-catching modified example. It was commissioned by *4x4 Mart* magazine in 2003 as the first prize in a national competition. The whole project, including buying the donor vehicle, came in at exactly £5,000. *(Author)*

Below: The team behind Midlands-based Suzi Q's, a bunch of Suzuki 4x4 fanatics and experts offer vehicles for sale, a vast array of accessories, MoT and servicing facilities, and a full paint shop and bodywork repair centre. *(Author)*

Bottom: Suzi Q's accessories store has something for everyone wanting to turn their Suzuki 4x4 into an attention-grabbing street car. Stocks are impressive, and a full fitting service is also available on-site. *(Author)*

the crowd. The end result was distinctive and attractive, and all achieved without breaking the bank; in fact, the entire project – including the cost of the donor vehicle – came in at a very reasonable £5,000 back then. It just goes to show what can be achieved without going overboard with your credit cards.

4x4 Mart was keen to boast about its latest competition prize:

'This particular Vitara comes with stainless-steel bull bar, side steps, spare wheel surround and sill covers,' they explained. 'It's also got a chrome exhaust tail pipe, chrome numberplate surrounds, impressive alloys and extra-wide tyres. This is a Vitara Verdi for those who like to get noticed, that's for sure. Apart from all that, our little Vit also comes with a recent full service, a new cam belt and a thorough check-over courtesy of the guys at Suzi Q's. It's recently been issued with a fresh MoT – which, naturally, it passed without problem.'

Despite the fact that they were giving away a nine-year-old 4x4, this proved to be one of *4x4 Mart*'s most successful competitions, such was the readers' enthusiasm for the vehicle. It all went to prove that, no matter how old the donor vehicle, a well-modified and

Above: Here's one that attracts plenty of attention: a Vitara Verdi with colour-coded hood, tubular side steps and a very distinctive and dramatic looking front bull bar. Not everyone wants this kind of 'aggressive' look though. *(Author)*

Below: Wide arches, wide alloys and wide rubber; this is one of the ultimate Vitaras for the 'wide boy' buyer! *(Author)*

Above: Rather more subtle than most modified Vitaras is this smart and effective 1995 three-door hard-top, complete with chrome wheelarch edges and a simple chrome bull bar. It's not outrageous, but it looks cool. *(Author)*

Below: While the off-road fraternity raise their suspensions to cope with what mother nature throws at them, the 'street machine' crowd are known for dropping theirs! This expensively modified five-door Vitara is about as low as anyone has gone so far... *(Author)*

Left: If you want to upgrade the wheels and/or tyres on your Vitara, there's certainly no shortage of options on the market. It's important though, to bear in mind your main reason for owning the vehicle: is it an off-road workhorse or an on-road everyday car? This will hugely affect your final choice of tyres. *(Author)*

Above: White was a popular colour choice for Vitaras in the 1990s, and now makes an excellent base for an eye-catching 'street car'. With its extra-wide arches and ultra-fat three-spoke alloys, this example looks superb. *(Author)*

Below: This is simply wild! You don't need to go quite this far to create a seriously capable Vitara off-roader, though. With its body and suspension lift and virtually a complete re-engineering job to its credit, this particular Vitara is an awesome sight ... and incredibly capable in the rough, too. *(John Richardson)*

smartly presented Vitara is still more than capable of turning heads and attracting attention.

Suzi Q's, of course, isn't the only company offering a large range of accessories and improvements for Vitaras and other Suzukis. In fact, there are 4x4 specialists just about everywhere who are equally happy to look after your needs; a list of the major ones can be found in Appendix A. So, whether your on-road requirements are all about enhanced looks, improved handling, better brakes or simply a bit more 'oomph', you'll find an all-wheel drive specialist somewhere that is offering exactly what you want.

For Suzuki-owning people who never venture away from tarmac, most of the improvements tend to be based upon transforming a lowly standard model into a thing of beauty. For the off-road fraternity though, a completely different set of priorities suddenly comes into the equation…

In the rough

For the increasing number of enthusiasts who like nothing more than to put their Suzuki 4x4 through its off-road paces, there's plenty of choice of vehicles available. As we saw in Chapter Six, there's a second-hand Suzuki for just about everyone, no matter how limited a budget.

Once you've bought your ideal off-road Suzuki, you probably want to embark upon a series of modifications to help make it even better 'in the rough'. How far you go with these mods though, depends on how much time and money you want to spend on the project, as well as how seriously you're likely to be taking your off-roading.

There is absolutely no reason why you shouldn't take any SJ, Vitara, Jimny or whatever, off-road and have a lot of fun in it, without carrying out any modifications whatsoever. But if you're likely to be off-roading on a regular basis, some basic changes are certainly advisable.

For a start, have a look at the tyres on your vehicle. Are they the standard road tyres you'll find on most Suzukis? If so, they are likely to prove less than impressive in off-road conditions. You need maximum grip, and a standard set of rubber just isn't up to the job. Talk to some of the 4x4 specialist companies listed in Appendix A and ask them what the optimum choice of tyre is for your model. Tell them how much of your driving is likely to be off-road; how important (or not!) on-road comfort is to you; and also what kind of a budget you have to play with. They will then be able to come up with the ideal

compromise for your needs. It's not rocket science, but the perfect choice of tyre will vary between different vehicles and different owners. Get the right set of rubber on your vehicle and, you will be amazed at the difference in grip and go-anywhere capabilities.

Off-road tyres will get you to places you couldn't have reached beforehand, but you don't want to ruin your engine getting there. That's why an engine snorkel of some description is advisable for serious off-roading. This ensures the air intake for your vehicle is higher than any water you are likely to be wading through, which is handy when it comes to preventing your engine from seizing up! That's why you see lots of off-roaders around with snorkels running up the side of their windscreens; you can't be too careful. Enthusiast John Richardson, writing for *4x4 Mart* magazine in 2003, was rather entertaining when describing his attitude towards off-road snorkels for his own SJ413:

'There are plenty of nice (and some not so nice) proprietary kits on the market, but those who followed my previous Vitara series will know what's coming. The choice is either £150 for a nice-looking kit or £25 for a bit of drainpipe from B&Q and a splash of imagination. Personally, for an out-and-out off-roader I can't see any point in spending that sort of cash on something that stands a good chance of being crushed or torn off, so off to B&Q we go.'

Despite the availability of very affordable early Vitaras these days, the good old SJ series is still being modded and upgraded by off-road fanatics. This SJ413 is a perfect example; even just a basic suspension lift and the addition of an engine snorkel will transform any SJ, Santana or Samurai into a very capable machine. *(John Richardson)*

WHAT THE PRESS SAID: Modifying an SJ413

'For any rabid Land Rover owners reading this, don't despair. Have a look under an SJ and you won't feel too alienated. Think 'Series Landie', now shrink it a bit and shed a few hundred pounds. There, that's better isn't it? On some models you'll even find a Santana Land Rover VIN plate! I personally started down the off-road route with an old Landie – as did most people I know – but after my first go in an SJ there was no looking back. Take off your blinkers and come and try one; you might just be surprised.' *(4x4 Mart, June 2003)*

Above: Exterior roll cage, snorkel, all-terrain tyres, raised suspension – the typical hallmarks of a Vitara created for life in the rough. This kind of heavily modified Suzuki will give most Land Rovers a run for their money when the going gets tough. *(John Richardson)*

Below: We warned you that going off-road could get your Suzuki a bit muddy! With the right kind of mods though, this type of terrain will prove no barrier to a well-driven Vitara. The light weight of most Suzuki 4x4s gives them an instant advantage in this kind of mud compared with the bigger, heavier vehicles they're often up against. *(John Richardson)*

The end result of a home-made snorkel may not look as professional as an off-the-shelf item, but for off-roading on a budget it certainly suffices. As for John Richardson, he was pretty philosophical about the finished job when he explained: 'And there we have it. An SJ with its own guttering. So just for all of you who think us so-called experts in magazines always get things right, take heart. It looks like crap. It'll keep the water out for now, but when I replace the wing it will almost certainly get binned.' It all depends how fussy you are about the aesthetics of your off-roader, I suppose.

So, with your off-road tyres and your newly built/acquired engine snorkel in place, you're much more prepared for some serious off-roading than you were before. Which means there's every chance you'll leave the rest of your vehicle as it is. Except, of course, you won't; because as soon as you see what some other folk get up to with theirs, you'll be wanting to follow suit. This is the start of a serious new addiction in your life, believe me.

Onward and upward

To decide what makes truly worthwhile off-road improvements, we need to look at the make-up of the average Suzuki 4x4 and where its few drawbacks lie. First though, the good news.

If talking of SJs, Jimnys and three-door Vitaras, we're dealing with vehicles that offer short wheelbases, very little front and rear overhang and the versatility of a dual-range transfer box. We also have lightweight designs that are adept at 'floating' over mud where heavier vehicles get bogged down, and we have the advantages of relatively straightforward engineering which isn't too difficult to upgrade where necessary.

The short wheelbase of such a Suzuki means less likelihood of getting 'grounded' on the apex of a steep hill than if we were piloting something far larger; it doesn't negate the risk completely though. That's why plenty of off-road Suzuki drivers opt for raised suspension and body lifts. This will obviously give extra ground clearance, will reduce the chances of becoming 'grounded' and helps when wading through deep water or mud. It also frees up enough space to fit some monstrous tyres, if that's what you want. But just how is this achieved?

Companies like LA Supertrux and KAP Suzuki (more of whom later) will happily carry out a body lift conversion for you, endowing your SJ, Vitara or

Anyone who's serious about off-roading will do well to invest in an electric winch for hauling themselves out of trouble or for tackling the steepest inclines imaginable. At the very least, a strong tow rope is essential; then all you need is some help from another 4x4er! *(John*

A couple of SJs parked nose-to-nose give an idea of the difference that suspension and body lifts can make. This is the kind of mod that comes into its own when wading through water or tackling ultra-steep slopes. *(John Richardson)*

Jimny with an extra three or four inches on average. And that's enough to enable you to squeeze up to 30-inch tyres beneath the vehicle – the kind of rubber that many an aspiring off-road driver's dreams are made of. A body lift combined with serious suspension upgrades will also enable you to achieve potentially fantastic axle articulation; your Suzuki then suddenly becomes unstoppable in even the most unforgiving terrain.

How a body lift works is, in principle, very simple. The idea is to put some kind of a spacer between the body mounts and the chassis mounting points. Many of the kits available are of similar design and the job itself isn't too difficult if you're a practical sort with a reasonable tool kit. Be prepared to have to carry out one or two extra modifications as a result of the lift though, such as rearranging the brake pipes. And don't forget you're increasing the vehicle's centre of gravity too, which will obviously have an effect on tarmac-style handling – although with the chassis and running gear staying relatively low, this is probably less noticeable than you might expect.

Arguably the best of the body lifts is the kind of kit that uses a combination of steel box sections and aluminium or graphite block spacers. These tend to use the original nuts, mounts and bushes for simplicity; they are easily accessible for maintenance and checkovers, and they can be simply removed and used on another vehicle when the time comes to swap your Suzuki for another.

Shackle reversal kits are another popular way of getting your Suzuki heading skywards. These consist of either weld-on or bolt-on turrets that enable the swing shackles to be mounted on the inner rather than the outer spring mounts. Ride quality improvements can be a useful and pleasantly surprising side-effect of this conversion, although serious 'brake dive' when trying to stop quickly at speed is a reputed downside. This isn't the neatest type of conversion around, either; in fact, there are some far better options available.

One of the most effective ways of raising the height (particularly of a Vitara) is a straightforward suspension lift, usually of between 1.5 and three inches. Pro Comp offer a 1.5in spring lift, but many owners demand more. An excellent example of a 3in lift kit is made by Calmini in the States and sold in the UK via Specialist Leisure; it's not outrageously difficult to fit, although many owners prefer to leave the job to a specialist rather than tackle it at home. As with so many tasks, much depends on your own capabilities as a DIY mechanic.

Dramatic suspension lifts demand longer-than-standard springs and shock absorbers, with Explorer Pro Comp ES3000s being popular and reliable choices. This then frees up enough space underneath your Suzuki to get some serious rubber in place. It's a perfect example of how what looks like a singular modification leads to several others becoming necessary along the way.

Another increasingly popular conversion is 'SPOA' (spring over axle), an idea with its origins in the USA.

This essentially involves fabricating and welding new spring seats and saddles to allow a Suzuki's leaf springs to be fitted above the axle casing, although a range of specific bolt-on kits is now available.

Advantages of this principle include its relative simplicity, as well as the fact that – if you wish – you can retain your Suzuki's original shock absorbers. This makes SPOA a cost-effective option for owners on limited budgets. Bear in mind though, that it can put extra strain on your springs and can therefore reduce their life expectancy, as well as having something of an adverse effect on your steering. Still, it's an idea worth considering.

With a body lift, upgraded suspension and seriously large tyres, any modified Suzuki is going to be a competent and competitive off-road machine. But just how far do you really want (or need) to go? Always be honest with yourself about how much off-roading you are likely to be doing over the next year or so, and whether the cost implications of a professional conversion actually make sense. Take into account your own capabilities too, and whether you'll

be off-roading in a competitive sense. If, as far as you're concerned, it's all about fun rather than outright competition, you can get away with a lot less than briefly explained here – and still have a fantastic time in the process.

Going further . . .

Unless your Vitara has already been modified before you bought it, it is more than likely it doesn't have a limited slip rear differential (LSD) fitted. If not, it is certainly worth considering if you're intent on transforming your vehicle into more than just an occasional off-roader. In simple terms, a rear LSD will prevent your rear wheels from rotating at different speeds. Therefore, if one wheel finds itself in a particularly sticky situation that would ordinarily have it spinning wildly and not getting anywhere, an LSD means it will now rotate at the same speed as the other rear wheel and will therefore haul itself out of trouble.

Some special edition Vitaras (like the fairly rare X-EC) came with rear LSD as standard, although various aftermarket alternatives are available from 4x4 specialists everywhere. Costs will vary, so it pays to shop around, but the end result could be well worthwhile if you take your off-roading seriously.

You might also want to consider a roll cage for your vehicle, depending on the type of off-road use you anticipate. It's particularly important with something like a soft-top SJ or Samurai; get one of these into a serious roll and you will find the whole structure alarmingly weak. What is more important: the extra expense of a roll cage or the prospect of being seriously injured or even killed? Internal and external roll cages are available for most of the popular Suzuki off-roaders, and it is a purchase that is highly recommended.

While on the subject of extra off-road equipment, don't forget to stock up on essentials to get yourself out of trouble when you're out 'in the rough'. At the very least, you will need some decent boots, a pair of

Above, left: Big rubber, raised body, and uprated suspension. This superbly prepared Vitara Soft Top is all set for its next bout of fun in the mud. *(John Richardson)*

Left: There's no shortage of 'mud terrain' tyres on the market, although the various types produced by BF Goodrich are a popular choice. They're good value, they wear well and they give fantastic grip in most conditions. *(John Richardson)*

Above: When your off-road tyres accumulate this much mud, they lose a great deal of their grip. It's a good idea to hose them down before embarking on the next stage of your all-terrain day in the rough...
(John Richardson)

Below: If you fail to fit an engine snorkel to your Suzuki before you embark on this kind of 'water splash', you're bound to regret it afterwards. A simple snorkel enables you to tackle surprisingly deep water without flooding your engine or causing any major damage. It's one of those essential off-road modifications. *(John Richardson)*

gloves, wheel-changing equipment, a good quality tow rope, some spare fuel, a full water container and a basic tool kit which includes spare fuses, wire, bulbs, a can of WD40, and so on. Failing to prepare yourself in such a way is foolhardy, to say the least. When off-roading in a group or taking part in a 4x4 fun day, there is usually plenty of help around from other willing volunteers, but don't assume there will always be someone else nearby with a tow rope or a tool kit you can use.

One final point about equipment: many off-road Suzuki owners are now fitting electric front winches to their vehicles. This is an excellent idea if you're going to be off-roading most weekends and likely to be pushing your vehicle to the limit. Being able to winch yourself up a crazily steep incline or out of a mud bath that proved more than a match for your vehicle can be both useful and pretty good fun. It makes you more self-sufficient too, should there be a lack of help available. Do shop around though, and talk to 4x4 specialists about the ideal winch for your particular needs; prices and specifications vary greatly, with companies such as Warn offering a wide range of winches to suit all pockets. Do your homework thoroughly; you might just avoid spending more money than you need to.

Heading off-road

I'm not going into intricate detail here about the various types of off-road competitions that exist for those already heavily involved in the sport. Whether you're into trialling or comp safari events, you will already have spent a serious amount of money preparing your vehicle, you will be a member of one or more of the various clubs which organise the sports, and you will have gone much further in the preparation of your Suzuki than most readers of this book.

For the rest of us though, who tend to look upon off-roading as a non-competitive fun activity for the weekend, there are now lots of new opportunities to get our Suzukis dirty. More off-road driving schools than ever before have been established throughout the UK, and 4x4 fun days are becoming increasingly popular too.

How the latter work is very simple. You turn up on the day at a specially designated site (often an old quarry), you pay your fee (usually between £30 and £45), you sign a disclaimer (acknowledging that you and you alone are responsible for your vehicle and your own personal safety) … and then you spend the next few hours having fun.

First-timers at most 4x4 fun days will find help and advice available to them if they so wish. An expert will usually be available to give you basic instruction on off-roading, and they will often accompany you on a trip round the course if you ask them to, so you can get acquainted with the layout and what's on offer.

The whole point about off-road fun days is that there's no competition involved. The only person you're up against (in terms of how hard you push your vehicle) is yourself. Whether you're the kind of owner who wants to potter round the perimeter of the site and practice on the easy sections, or are the more adventurous fanatic who likes nothing more than powering your SJ through a lake just for the sheer hell of it, you will be made equally welcome at any such event.

There's no competition, no prizes and no winners; you're there just to have fun. If that's what you're into, do make sure it is either as part of a properly organised fun day or, if you're 'going your own way', you have the land owner's full permission. There's a lot of controversy at the time of writing about off-roaders using 'green lanes' and other public spaces to put their vehicles through their paces, much to the annoyance of ramblers, cyclists, horse riders and the like. Whatever we may individually think about such opinions, we all need to be aware of other land users. In recent years, less-responsible 4x4 owners have helped to spoil the reputation of off-roaders amongst the public at large.

That is why I personally recommend 4x4 fun days as the ideal compromise, and by talking to companies such as 4x4 Funday Ltd, you will be able to find out what's coming up in your area over the next few months. Go on, have fun!

KAP Suzuki

We can't leave a chapter on Suzuki modifications without mentioning KAP Suzuki, a Yorkshire-based company founded by Suzuki fanatic Darren Wilson. 'We can supply any amount of spares, from a bolt to a full vehicle,' Darren explains. 'And from our fully stocked breaker's yard we can supply parts for SJ410, SJ413, Samurai, Vitara and Jimny.'

Darren is a particular fan of the Jimny and has created a number of very special examples over the years, the most exciting of which have been used successfully in comp safari events. These highly modified Jimnys can be seen at some of the biggest 4x4 shows each year, providing excellent publicity for Darren and his company.

As Jimnys continue to become more affordable on the second-hand market, Darren finds increasing numbers of owners coming to him for help and advice. In no time at all, they're able to see their vehicles transformed into truly rugged, go-anywhere off-roaders capable of showing any standard Land Rover how it should be done. Darren has his own team of experts and fanatics working with him in the company's modern, well-equipped workshops. And what they manage to create is often quite amazing…

If you prefer to do the work yourself, that's no problem either. Darren will happily supply anything from his vast range of SJ and Jimny off-road accessories and equipment, particular favourites amongst his customers being longer spring sets (two to three inches), toughened transfer box mounts, modified fuel tanks (from 4.5 to eight gallons), five to eight-inch spot lamps, internal roll cages and vented front brake discs.

To find out more, contact Darren Wilson or take a look at KAP Suzuki's website; full details can be found in Appendix A.

Chapter Ten

Looking after your Suzuki

As this book covers numerous Suzuki models, between them employing a wide array of separate powerplants, it's impossible to offer here a definitive guide to maintaining and servicing every version. For a more detailed approach, you're advised to consult the relevant Haynes Service and Repair Manual for your particular model; there you'll find a plethora of more specific advice and step-by-step guides.

Having said that, much of the basic maintenance of an all-wheel-drive Suzuki applies equally to other 4x4s, so I'll attempt to deal with as much of this as possible.

Keeping your Suzuki in excellent condition throughout will pay dividends when it comes to future resale value. Although this Jimny has been used occasionally off-road, it has been thoroughly cleaned after each 'outing'. *(Author)*

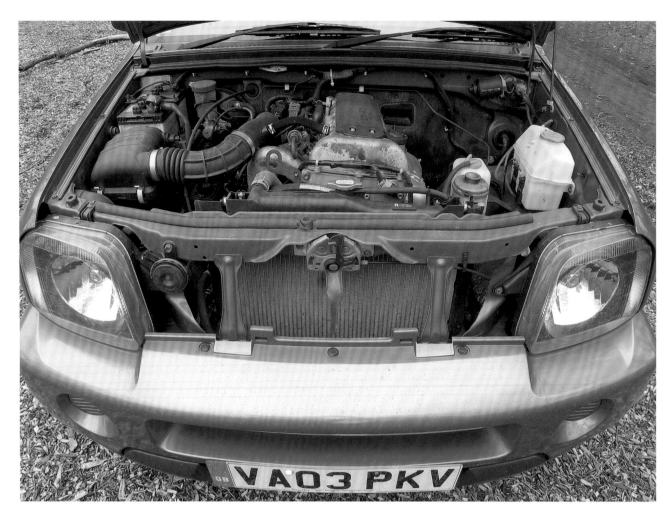

Routine maintenance

The most obvious advice when talking about basic maintenance is: do make sure you adhere to the manufacturer's recommended service intervals. This applies as much to a well-worn SJ as it does to a nearly new Grand Vitara; whatever the age or spec of your Suzuki, regular servicing is an absolute must, and particularly if you're a keen off-roader.

Fail to change the oil in your engine when you should, for example, and over time you will find yourself up against premature engine wear and extra long-term expense. Also, if you're an avid off-road fan and like nothing more than pushing your Suzuki to the limit 'in the rough', you'll find yourself going through sets of brake pads, alternators, batteries and the like far more frequently than the average tarmac-only motorist. Although Suzukis tend to be inherently reliable, any kind of hard off-road work puts extra pressure on key components, which means more regular checks and maintenance should soon become second nature to you.

Much of the basic maintenance that goes with regular off-roading boils down to common sense. In extreme off-road conditions, for example, it's not unusual for radiators to get caked in mud which, once dried, hugely restricts airflow and can cause overheating, which in turn can cause major engine damage if left unchecked. The simple answer is to keep your radiator as clean as possible with regular jet-washing, which will help prolong the life of both the radiator and everything else affected by the cooling system. In fact, keeping the whole of your under-bonnet area clean and free from any serious build-up of mud will be beneficial in the long run.

A good hosing down of your brakes is important after off-roading, too. A build-up of sand or mud will not only make your brakes less effective and potentially dangerous on the road, but can also deeply score your brake discs. Go off-roading in an old quarry, for example, and you may find the dust there is very abrasive and damaging. The sooner you can remove all traces of it afterwards, the more your Suzuki will benefit.

Opposite: Keeping your under-bonnet area clean and tidy shows a well-cared-for vehicle. It also makes the weekly maintenance checks a bit more pleasurable! *(Author)*

Right: Suzukis are designed with ease of maintenance in mind with most of the essentials tending to be easily accessible for even the least technically minded of owners. *(Author)*

Below: A tatty, torn or just plain dirty hood will have an adverse effect on the resale value of any used Suzuki soft-top. This Vitara has been treated to a new hood, which is a great plus-point when selling. But you may not need to go that far – keep your hood clean and it will pay dividends later on. *(Author)*

Opposite, top left: Going off-road? It's easy to forget to check things like your washer bottle fluid level, even though you're likely to need this more than ever 'in the rough'. *(Author)*

Opposite, top right: Unless you're going to extremes in terms of modifications, your Suzuki's standard electrical system should be able to cope with sensible changes. *(Author)*

Opposite, bottom: The interiors of soft-top Suzukis can suffer from condensation, particularly in the UK during the winter months. This in turn can lead to mould and mildew on upholstery and other surfaces. Keeping your interior clean and giving the seats and trim a wipe-over with a damp cloth every so often will help to keep your interior pristine. *(Author)*

While you're out with your jet wash, don't forget to make full use of it underneath your Suzuki, too. A regular build-up of mud will often cause bodywork problems later on; most Suzukis have a whole host of mud traps and 'nooks and crannies' just waiting to catch debris, moisture and whatever else off-roading

Buying an elderly Vitara? Suzuki recommended a service every 6,000 miles on early examples. By the time the Jimny arrived a decade later, 9,000-mile intervals had become the norm. *(Author)*

throws at them. Neglect the underside and, eventually, you'll find rust setting in – a subject we'll come to a little further on in this chapter.

We've previously talked about the importance of buying a Suzuki with a full service history; well, the continuation of this history is equally vital once you've bought your vehicle. Even if you choose to use a small independent garage rather than a Suzuki-franchised dealer for your maintenance and servicing, there's no reason why they can't keep your service book up to date and stamped. When you come to sell your Suzuki, it will be well worthwhile; buyers are always impressed by evidence of regular servicing and a high standard of maintenance.

When going through any vehicle's history, don't forget to check when (or indeed, if) it last had its cam belt changed. If you've already acquired the vehicle and

Above: When having your Suzuki serviced, don't forget to have the service book stamped up-to-date. Even if it's a non-Suzuki dealer doing the work, it will still show future buyers of your car that it has been well maintained. *(Author)*

Left: Keeping the underside of your wheelarches and the underneath of your 4x4 this clean isn't easy if you use it regularly off-road. Regular jet-washing though, will help to keep any accumulation of mud to an absolute minimum. *(Author)*

you can find no record of a new cam belt, don't delay: get your vehicle booked in for the job as soon as possible. If the worst happens and your cam belt snaps, you'll be very lucky to escape with anything less than a full engine rebuild or even a replacement. If you're thinking of buying a Suzuki that hasn't yet had its cam belt changed, make sure you budget this into the price when negotiating with the vendor.

Bodywork care

Previous chapters have already dealt with the fact that elderly Suzuki 4x4s do rust. They're made from steel, after all, and they're not going to last for ever. There is

The front edge of a Jimny's bonnet is particularly vulnerable to stone chips. Check regularly for these, and make sure they're properly 'touched-up' before they have a chance to rust. *(Author)*

Is rust taking a hold on your Suzuki? If it's structural, it will affect your vehicle's ability to pass its next MoT test. If it's purely cosmetic, it needs dealing with if it's not to become even more unsightly. This corrosion on the front wing of a Samurai was all that was wrong bodily with this particular example – and it didn't cost its owner much to put right. *(Author)*

Below: Suzuki 4x4 upholstery isn't renowned for being long lasting or particularly robust. This is how an SJ seat looked after just 65,000 miles. However, on a vehicle of such low value, it isn't worth having a professional repair carried out. In this case, a pair of aftermarket seat covers created a cheap and effective makeover! *(Author)*

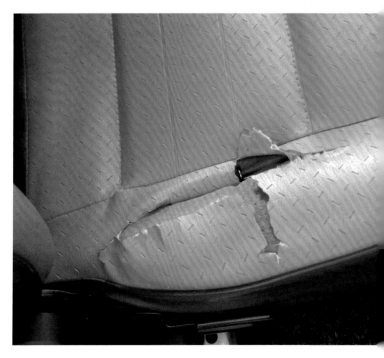

much that you, as an owner, can do to at least slow down the corrosion process, though.

For a start, think about investing in a DIY pressure washer if you haven't already got one. These needn't be expensive, yet they're hugely useful to anybody who owns a 4x4 that leads an active life.

Whenever you head off-road and encounter the usual combination of mud, water, slurry, sand and the like, use your pressure washer when you get home to remove as much of this as you can before it dries hard. You only need to glance underneath your Suzuki to realise there's no shortage of areas where such debris can become trapped: all around the chassis members; up inside the wheelarches; behind light units; around box sections ... and a whole lot more.

Combine this with the corrosive road salt that local councils drop on the streets every winter and you have an undesirable cocktail of rust-inducing 'rubbish' accumulated under your vehicle.

If you're very keen, you might even want to think about investing in some kind of rust-prevention treatment. Products such as Waxoyl can be applied either by brush or sprayed into hard-to-reach places to remove moisture, apply an anti-corrosive layer that never dries out, and slow down any rusting that may already have started. It can be time and money well spent, depending on how long you intend keeping your vehicle.

The weight of a spare wheel permanently mounted on a side-hinged rear tailgate can cause premature wear in the hinges. Check there's no 'drop' when you open the back door. *(Author)*

Inside story

Owners of off-road LJs and SJs won't find this section of the chapter particularly useful, as they are unlikely to be worried about the condition and maintenance of their vehicle's interior. For the rest of us though, how we treat the insides of our cars can have a significant effect on residuals when the time comes to sell.

Again, it is not exactly rocket science, so I won't insult you by suggesting that you empty your ashtray every so often and vacuum your carpets from time to time; if, however, you intend taking your Suzuki off-road at all, I would suggest you spend some money on full-width protective mats for your floor and a set of protective vinyl covers for your seats. You might think it's only the outside of your car that gets muddy when you drive off-road, but it isn't. At some point you will want to get out of your vehicle, chat with other owners, see what other drivers are getting up to in the mud – and as soon as you climb back inside, you'll be taking all that 'crud' in with you. And, make no mistake, ex-quarry mud on your carpets or smeared onto your seats is very difficult indeed to remove properly.

Have a chat with one or two of the 4x4 specialist retailers listed in Appendix A and see what they have to offer in terms of interior protection. Spend a few pounds before you head for the mud and, I promise you, it will be a wise investment.

Careful driving

When it comes to looking after any 4x4, one area of concern which many people overlook is that of driving style, and this is particularly so when it comes to off-roading. How you drive your Suzuki can have a major impact on its longevity, reliability and resale value, yet many owners underestimate this vital fact.

Again, I'm not going to stand in judgement and preach about how you should behave when you're behind the wheel, but what I would suggest is that, particularly when it comes to off-road driving, you at least adopt a degree of 'mechanical sympathy'.

Let's take the basic example of Suzuki's dual-range transfer box. Although the principle behind the company's part-time all-wheel drive set-up has changed relatively little over the years, the transfer box itself has been developed. Buy a Jimny or Grand Vitara nowadays and you will find you no longer need to bring your vehicle to a complete standstill in order to select high-ratio four-wheel drive from two-wheel drive. In fact, Suzuki claim you can do so at any speed up to 100kmh (62mph). But is this really wise? My argument is, why put extra strain on your transfer box and transmission unnecessarily simply to prove a point? Bring your speed down to a more sensible level, then select '4H' and I'm convinced you'll be doing the whole system a big favour. You are then more likely to be enjoying trouble-free motoring for a long time to come.

Keeping your interior clean can be an arduous task if you're a regular off-roader. It's a good idea to invest in some plastic seat covers and carpet protectors when you head off-road. It will save a lot of elbow grease in the long run! *(Author)*

Above: Looking for more luggage space from your Suzuki, or maybe you just want to keep your interior as new? A roof box like this can be a good idea for when going on family holidays. *(Suzuki GB)*

Opposite, top: Whether driving on the road or away from the tarmac, be prepared. A basic tool kit, warning triangle, strong tow rope and waterproof clothing should always be kept on board for emergencies. *(Frank Westworth)*

Opposite, bottom: Keep an eye on your tyre tread depth as part of your regular maintenance routine. A weekly check of your tyre pressures is vital too; if incorrect, it can lead to premature tyre wear as well as adversely affecting braking and handling. *(Author)*

An awareness of 'mechanical sympathy' makes for good, effective off-road driving in general. When tackling a steep downward slope, for example, off-road experts recommend you rely on engine braking rather than traditional braking, as this reduces the risk of skidding or going off course. (Bear in mind though, that a big-torque diesel-engined Grand Vitara will have much more engine braking at its disposal than a high-revving little SJ…) This certainly saves brake wear, and by letting your engine 'do the work' with no acceleration on your part, you're reducing its wear and tear in general.

When driving off-road, avoiding any drastic or sudden manoeuvres will help reduce the risk of mechanical damage. It's always tempting to aim for the roughest section of a track, the steepest part of an incline, the deepest area of a lake or the rockiest section of a course, but don't forget you're risking both mechanical and bodywork damage as a result.

If you're relying on your 4x4 to get you to work the next morning, it's a point worth remembering.

No wonder so many enthusiasts nowadays own old Suzukis purely and simply for off-road fun, with other cars employed as daily drivers. It's an ideal compromise, allowing them to 'go wild' in the mud at weekends and still have reliable everyday transport on Monday morning.

That's why half-decent SJs and Samurais get snapped up as soon as they come on to the second-hand market these days. They provide a simple, inexpensive route into the off-road scene – and what could be better than that?

Ancillary items like the horn can be vulnerable if you're a regular off-roader. A Jimny's horn is located just behind the front grille, making it prone to water and off-road damage in extreme circumstances.
(Author)

Appendix A

Specialists, clubs and contacts

Specialists

SUZI Q'S
9 Brades Road, Oldbury, Warley, West Midlands B69 2DP.
Tel/Fax: 0121 544 0200. Email: info@suzi-q.co.uk Website:
www.suzi-q.co.uk
Sales of standard and modified Vitaras; large stocks of parts and accessories; full servicing, repair and MoT facilities.

KAP SUZUKI
Beecher Street, Keighley, West Yorkshire BD21 4AP. Tel: 01535
610840. Mobile: 07870 279606. Email: darrenwilson@beeb.net
Website: www.kapsuzuki4x4.co.uk
Specialists in the design, development and supply of parts for all Suzuki 4x4s. Modified vehicles built to order. All models breaking for spares.

SPECIALIST LEISURE
Unit D2, Taylor Business Park, Risley, Warrington, Cheshire WA3
6BH. Tel: 01925 768833. Fax: 01925 768866. Email:
info@specialist-leisure.co.uk Website: www.specialist-leisure.co.uk
Importers of 4x4 accessories, including items for Jimny, Vitara and Grand Vitara.

LA SUPERTRUX
18 Lanchester Way, Royal Oak Industrial Estate, Daventry,
Northamptonshire NN11 5PH. Tel: 01327 705456. Fax: 01327
871786. Website: www.supertrux.com
Suppliers of suspension and body lift kits, plus many more off-road accessories.

MOORLAND
Tel: 01723 882335. Fax: 01723 882375.
Specialists in all parts for SJs and Samurais.

BIRMINGHAM MOTOR PARTS
610A Coventry Road, Smallheath, Birmingham B10 0US.
Tel/Fax: 0121 766 6008. Email: sales@japanese4x4spares.co.uk
Website: www.japanese4x4spares.co.uk

Suppliers of new parts for all Japanese 4x4s, including SJ, Samurai and Grand Vitara.

ROAD & TRAIL
Church Road, Leverington, Nr Wisbech, Cambridgeshire PE13
5DE. Tel: 01945 465337. Fax: 01945 476421. Email:
road.trail@talk21.com Website: www.roadandtrail4x4.co.uk
Specialist 4x4 breakers; Suzuki SJs and parts usually in stock.

PRESTIGE AUTOTRIM PRODUCTS
Oak Tree Place, Expressway Business Park, Rock Ferry, Birkenhead
CH42 1NS. Tel: 0151 643 9555. Fax: 0151 643 9634. Email:
sales@prestigecarhoods.com Website: www.prestigecarhoods.com
Manufacturers of replacement hoods for SJ-series and Vitara soft-tops.

MASTER COVERS
Unit 6, The Slipway, Port Solent, Portsmouth PO6 4TJ. Tel: 023
9237 4739. Fax: 023 9221 0803.
Replacement soft-tops for Santana, Samurai and SJ soft-tops.

EXPLORER UK
Poplar Park, Cliff Lane, Lymm, Cheshire WA13 0TD. Tel: 01925
757588. Fax: 01925 755146. Email: sales@explorerprocomp.co.uk
Website: www.explorerprocomp.co.uk
Suppliers of suspension lift kits, replacement springs and damper upgrades.

WEST COAST OFF-ROAD CENTRE
Gorsey Lane, Banks, Southport. Tel: 01704 229014. Fax: 01704
232911.
Supplier of Ironman suspension upgrades Suzuki LJ, SJ and Vitara.

FORMULA 4X4
Stafford Road, Stone, Staffordshire ST15 0UN. Tel: 01785
811211. Fax: 01785 817788. Email: info@formula4x4.com
Website: www.formula4x4.com
Suppliers of general 4x4 accessories and upgrades.

4X4 ACCESSORIES & TYRES
Mercury Park, Leeming Bar Industrial Estate, Leeming Bar, North Yorkshire DL7 9UN. Tel: 01677 425555. Fax: 01677 425666. Email: sales@4x4accessoriesandtyres.com Website: www.4x4accessoriesandtyres.com
Suppliers of general 4x4 accessories. Wheels and tyres a speciality.

SCORPION RACING 4X4 CENTRE
Unit D, The Coppetts Centre, North Circular Road, London N12 0SH. Tel: 020 8211 4888. Fax: 020 8211 4999. Website: www.scorpion-racing.co.uk
Suppliers of standard and uprated 4x4 parts and accessories, including suspension and brake upgrades.

CLN
78–80 Church Street, Chalvey, Slough, Berkshire SL1 2PE. Tel: 01753 570112. Fax: 01753 570114. Email: info@cln.ltd.uk Website: www.cln.ltd.uk
Suppliers of 4x4 bull bars, styling accessories and spare wheel covers.

WARN WINCHES
Arbil Ltd, Providence Street, Lye, Stourbridge, West Midlands DY9 8HS. Tel: 01384 895700. Fax: 01384 898645. Website: www.arbil.co.uk
UK importers of American-built Warn winches and lifting gear.

BRONCO 4X4
25 Broad Street, Leek, Staffordshire ST13 5NX. Tel: 01538 398555. Fax: 01538 398333. Email: sales@bronco4x4.com Website: www.bronco4x4.com
Off-road wheel and tyre specialists.

EQUICAR 4X4
Athena Works, Meadow Lane, Coseley, Nr Wolverhampton, West Midlands WV14 9NQ. Tel: 01902 882883. Fax: 01902 882855. Email: sales@equicar4x4.co.uk Website: www.equicar4x4.co.uk
Specialist 4x4 breakers, usually with Suzukis and parts in stock.

SMJ PRODUCTS
Unit 5B, Stanningley Trading Estate, off Richardshaw Lane, Leeds LS28 6BZ. Tel: 0113 236 0396. Fax: 0113 261 2357.
Custom-made leaf springs to original or modified specification.

Clubs
THE SUZUKI RHINO CLUB
The Old Mill, 45 London Road, East Grinstead, East Sussex RH19 1AW.
Open to owners of all 4x4 Suzukis. Four magazines per year, plus access to special events and competition days.

THE ALL-WHEEL DRIVE CLUB
PO Box 186, Uckfield, East Sussex TN22 3YQ. Tel: 01825 731875. Website: www.awdc.co.uk
Founded in 1968, the AWDC welcomes all 4x4 owners and organises various off-road events. Free bi-monthly magazine for members.

JAPANESE 4X4 CLUB OF GB
Tel: 07890 069826. Email: jap4x4club@yahoo.co.uk Website: www.jap4x4club.com
Owners' club catering for all makes and models of Japanese off-roaders.

THE GREEN LANE ASSOCIATION
PO Box 48, Huntingdon, Cambridgeshire PE26 2YY. Email: membership@glass-uk.org Website: www.glass-uk.org
Organisation dedicated to preserving vehicular rights of way and promoting sensible driving in the countryside.

SCOTTISH OFF-ROAD CLUB
Pirn Hill Farmhouse, Muthill, Perthshire PH5 2BP. Website: www.sorc.org.uk
Organises club events and off-road days throughout Scotland.

Off-road events organisers
4X4 FUNDAY
The Beeches, Llanidloes, Powys SY18 6EP. Tel: 01686 413151. Fax: 01686 413040. Email: richard@4x4funday.co.uk Website: www.4x4funday.co.uk
Organisers of non-competitive off-road fun days in Warwickshire, Worcestershire, Shropshire and Lancashire. Typical costs start at £30 per vehicle per day.

MOTOR SAFARI
Unit 230B, Redwither Central, Redwither Business Park, Wrexham, Clwyd LL13 9UE. Tel: 01978 754533. Fax: 01978 754534. Email: info@motor-safari.co.uk Website: www.motor-safari.co.uk
Off-road adventure driving and green laning at venues throughout the UK.

TRAILMASTERS INTERNATIONAL
Tel: 01691 649194. Email: info@trailmasters.com Website: www.trailmasters.com
Organisers of overseas off-road safaris and UK-based 4x4 weekends.

LANGDALE QUEST
Bickley Rigg Farm, Bickley, Langdale End, Scarborough, North Yorkshire YO13 0LL. Tel: 01723 882335. Fax: 01723 882375. Email: info@langdalequest.co.uk Website: www.langdalequest.co.uk
10,000-acre off-road centre, claimed to be the largest of its kind in the UK.

Global Suzuki

OFFICIAL WEBSITES FOR SUZUKI THROUGHOUT THE
WORLD:

Australia – www.suzuki.com.au
Austria – www.suzuki.at
Belgium – www.suzuki.be
Brazil – www.suzuki.com.br
Canada – www.suzuki.ca
Denmark – www.suzuki.dk
Egypt – www.seoudi.com/suzuki
Finland – www.suzuki.fi
France – www.suzuki.fr
Germany – www.suzuki.de
Greece – www.suzuki.gr
Hungary – www.suzuki.hu
Iceland – www.suzukibilar.is

India – www.marutiudyog.com
Ireland – www.suzuki.ie
Italy – www.suzuki.it
Japan – www.suzuki.co.jp
Netherlands – www.suzuki.nl
New Zealand – www.suzuki.co.nz
Norway – www.suzuki.no
Poland – www.suzuki.com.pl
Portugal – www.suzuki.cimpomovel.pt
Russia – www.suzuki-motor.ru
Spain – www.suzuki.es
Sweden – www.suzuki.se
Thailand – www.thaisuzuki.co.th
Turkey – www.suzuki.com.tr
UK – www.suzuki.co.uk
USA – www.suzuki.com

Appendix B

Technical specifications

Suzuki LJ80

ENGINE:	797cc OHC 8-valve four-cylinder
MAX POWER:	41bhp @ 5,500rpm
MAX TORQUE:	44lb ft @ 3,500rpm
PERFORMANCE:	Max speed approx. 70mph
ECONOMY:	Approx. 40mpg
TRANSMISSION:	Four-speed manual
DRIVE:	Part-time four-wheel drive; dual-range transfer box
STEERING:	Non-assisted recirculating ball and nut
BRAKES:	Drums all round
SUSPENSION:	Front struts; rear leaf springs
OVERALL LENGTH:	3,185mm
OVERALL WIDTH:	1,395mm
OVERALL HEIGHT:	1,685mm (LJ80V)
WHEELBASE:	1,930mm
GROUND CLEARANCE:	240mm

Suzuki SJ410

ENGINE:	970cc OHC 8-valve four-cylinder
MAX POWER:	45bhp @ 5,500rpm
MAX TORQUE:	54lb ft @ 3,000rpm
PERFORMANCE:	Max speed approx. 74mph
ECONOMY:	27.2mpg (urban); 33.2mpg (at 56mph)
TRANSMISSION:	Four-speed manual
DRIVE:	Part-time four-wheel drive; dual-range transfer box
STEERING:	Non-assisted recirculating ball and nut
BRAKES:	Front discs; self-adjusting rear drums
SUSPENSION:	Live axles; semi-elliptic leaf springs; telescopic dampers
OVERALL LENGTH:	3,440mm
OVERALL WIDTH:	1,460mm
OVERALL HEIGHT:	1,690mm (SJ410V JL)
WHEELBASE:	2,030mm
GROUND CLEARANCE:	230mm

Suzuki Santana

ENGINE:	970cc OHC 8-valve four-cylinder
MAX POWER:	45bhp @ 5,500rpm
MAX TORQUE:	54lb ft @ 3,000rpm
PERFORMANCE:	Max speed approx. 79mph
ECONOMY:	30.4mpg (urban); 32.8mpg (at 56mph)
TRANSMISSION:	Five-speed manual
DRIVE:	Part-time four-wheel drive; dual-range transfer box
STEERING:	Non-assisted recirculating ball and nut
BRAKES:	Front discs; self-adjusting rear drums; servo assisted
SUSPENSION:	Live axles; semi-elliptic leaf springs; telescopic dampers
OVERALL LENGTH:	3,430mm
OVERALL WIDTH:	1,460mm
OVERALL HEIGHT:	1,680mm
WHEELBASE:	2,030mm
GROUND CLEARANCE:	230mm

Suzuki SJ413

ENGINE:	1,324cc all-alloy OHC 8-valve four-cylinder
MAX POWER:	63bhp @ 6,000rpm
MAX TORQUE:	73.7lb ft @ 3,500rpm
PERFORMANCE:	Max speed approx. 85mph
ECONOMY:	31.7mpg (urban); 35.7mpg (at 56mph); 33.6mpg (at 75mph)
TRANSMISSION:	Five-speed manual
DRIVE:	Part-time four-wheel drive; dual-range transfer box
STEERING:	Non-assisted recirculating ball and nut
BRAKES:	Front discs; self-adjusting rear drums; servo assisted
SUSPENSION:	Live axles; semi-elliptic leaf springs; telescopic dampers; anti-roll bar

OVERALL LENGTH:	3,440mm
OVERALL WIDTH:	1,460mm
OVERALL HEIGHT:	1,690mm
WHEELBASE:	2,030mm
GROUND CLEARANCE:	230mm

Suzuki Samurai

ENGINE:	1,298cc OHC 8-valve four-cylinder
MAX POWER:	68.3bhp @ 6,000rpm
MAX TORQUE:	76lb ft @ 3,500rpm
PERFORMANCE:	Max speed approx. 88mph
ECONOMY:	30.1mpg (urban); 37.2mpg (at 56mph); 30.5mpg (at 75mph)
TRANSMISSION:	Five-speed manual
DRIVE:	Part-time four-wheel drive; dual-range transfer box
STEERING:	Non-assisted recirculating ball and nut
BRAKES:	Front discs; self-adjusting rear drums; servo assisted
SUSPENSION:	Live axles; semi-elliptic leaf springs; telescopic dampers; anti-roll bar
OVERALL LENGTH:	3,430mm
OVERALL WIDTH:	1,530mm
OVERALL HEIGHT:	1,665mm
WHEELBASE:	2,030mm
GROUND CLEARANCE:	230mm

Suzuki Vitara 1.6i SWB 8-valve

ENGINE:	1,590cc OHC 8-valve four-cylinder; single-point fuel-injection
MAX POWER:	79bhp @ 5,400rpm
MAX TORQUE:	93.9lb ft @ 3,000rpm
PERFORMANCE:	Max speed approx. 88mph
ECONOMY:	28mpg (urban); 36.2mpg (at 56mph); 25.9mpg (at 75mph)
TRANSMISSION:	Five-speed manual
DRIVE:	Part-time four-wheel drive; dual-range transfer box
STEERING:	Power-assisted recirculating ball and nut
BRAKES:	Front discs; self-adjusting rear drums; servo assisted
SUSPENSION:	Front MacPherson struts; multi-link rear
OVERALL LENGTH:	3,620mm
OVERALL WIDTH:	1,630mm
OVERALL HEIGHT:	1,665mm
WHEELBASE:	2,200mm
GROUND CLEARANCE:	230mm

Suzuki Vitara 1.6i SWB 16-valve

ENGINE:	1,590cc OHC 16-valve four-cylinder; multi-point fuel-injection
MAX POWER:	95bhp @ 5,600rpm
MAX TORQUE:	97.6lb ft @ 4,000rpm
PERFORMANCE:	Max speed approx. 92mph
ECONOMY:	28.2mpg (urban); 38.2mpg (at 56mph); 25.4mpg (at 75mph)
TRANSMISSION:	Five-speed manual (optional four-speed automatic)
DRIVE:	Part-time four-wheel drive; dual-range transfer box
STEERING:	Power-assisted recirculating ball and nut
BRAKES:	Front discs; self-adjusting rear drums; servo assisted
SUSPENSION:	Front MacPherson struts; multi-link rear
OVERALL LENGTH:	3,620mm
OVERALL WIDTH:	1,630mm
OVERALL HEIGHT:	1,665mm
WHEELBASE:	2,200mm
GROUND CLEARANCE:	230mm

Suzuki Vitara 1.6i LWB 16-valve

ENGINE:	1,590cc OHC 16-valve four-cylinder; multi-point fuel-injection
MAX POWER:	95bhp @ 5,600rpm
MAX TORQUE:	97.6lb ft @ 4,000rpm
PERFORMANCE:	Max speed approx. 91mph
ECONOMY:	26.4mpg (urban); 36.7mpg (at 56mph); 27.2mpg (at 75mph)
TRANSMISSION:	Five-speed manual (optional four-speed automatic)
DRIVE:	Part-time four-wheel drive; dual-range transfer box
STEERING:	Power-assisted recirculating ball and nut
BRAKES:	Front discs; self-adjusting rear drums; servo assisted
SUSPENSION:	Front MacPherson struts; multi-link rear
OVERALL LENGTH:	4,030mm
OVERALL WIDTH:	1,630mm
OVERALL HEIGHT:	1,700mm
WHEELBASE:	2,480mm
GROUND CLEARANCE:	230mm

Suzuki Vitara 2.0 TD LWB

ENGINE:	2.0-litre turbocharged four-cylinder diesel with intercooler
MAX POWER:	71bhp @ 4,000rpm
MAX TORQUE:	N/A
PERFORMANCE:	Max speed approx. 83mph
ECONOMY:	Approx. 38–40mpg
TRANSMISSION:	Five-speed manual (optional four-speed automatic)
DRIVE:	Part-time four-wheel drive; dual-range transfer box
STEERING:	Power-assisted recirculating ball and nut
BRAKES:	Front discs; self-adjusting rear drums; servo assisted
SUSPENSION:	Front MacPherson struts; multi-link rear
OVERALL LENGTH:	4,030mm
OVERALL WIDTH:	1,630mm
OVERALL HEIGHT:	1,700mm
WHEELBASE:	2,480mm
GROUND CLEARANCE:	230mm

Suzuki Vitara 2.0 V6 LWB

ENGINE:	2.0-litre DOHC V6 petrol; multi-point fuel-injection
MAX POWER:	135bhp @ 5,200rpm
MAX TORQUE:	N/A
PERFORMANCE:	Max speed approx. 100mph
ECONOMY:	Approx. 23–26mpg
TRANSMISSION:	Five-speed manual (optional four-speed automatic)
DRIVE:	Part-time four-wheel drive; dual-range transfer box
STEERING:	Power-assisted recirculating ball and nut
BRAKES:	Front discs; self-adjusting rear drums; servo assisted
SUSPENSION:	Front MacPherson struts; multi-link rear
OVERALL LENGTH:	4,030mm
OVERALL WIDTH:	1,630mm
OVERALL HEIGHT:	1,700mm
WHEELBASE:	2,480mm
GROUND CLEARANCE:	230mm

Suzuki Jimny Hard Top

ENGINE:	1,298cc OHC/1328cc DOHC 16-valve fuel-injected four-cylinder
MAX POWER:	79bhp @ 6,000rpm/5,500rpm
MAX TORQUE:	76.7lb ft/81lb ft @ 4,500rpm
PERFORMANCE:	Max speed 88mph
ECONOMY:	27.7mpg (urban); 39.8mpg (extra urban); 34.4mpg (combined)
TRANSMISSION:	Five-speed manual (optional four-speed automatic)
DRIVE:	Part-time four-wheel drive; dual-range transfer box
STEERING:	Power-assisted recirculating ball and nut
BRAKES:	Front discs; self-adjusting rear drums; servo assisted
SUSPENSION:	Three-link rigid with coil springs
OVERALL LENGTH:	3,625mm
OVERALL WIDTH:	1,600mm
OVERALL HEIGHT:	1,705mm
WHEELBASE:	2,250mm
GROUND CLEARANCE:	190mm

Suzuki Jimny Soft Top

ENGINE:	1,298cc OHC 16-valve fuel-injected four-cylinder
MAX POWER:	79bhp @ 6,000rpm
MAX TORQUE:	76.7lb ft @ 4,500rpm
PERFORMANCE:	Max speed 88mph
ECONOMY:	32.1mpg (urban); 45.6mpg (extra urban); 39.2mpg (combined)
TRANSMISSION:	Five-speed manual (optional four-speed automatic)
DRIVE:	Part-time four-wheel drive; dual-range transfer box
STEERING:	Power-assisted recirculating ball and nut
BRAKES:	Front discs; self-adjusting rear drums; servo assisted
SUSPENSION:	Three-link rigid with coil springs
OVERALL LENGTH:	3,625mm
OVERALL WIDTH:	1,600mm
OVERALL HEIGHT:	1,655mm
WHEELBASE:	2,250mm
GROUND CLEARANCE:	190mm

Suzuki GV1600

ENGINE:	1,590cc 16-valve OHC four-cylinder; multi-point fuel-injection
MAX POWER:	92bhp @ 5,200rpm
MAX TORQUE:	101.9lb ft @ 4,000rpm
PERFORMANCE:	Max speed 93mph
ECONOMY:	28.2mpg (urban); 41.5mpg (extra urban); 35.3mpg (combined)
TRANSMISSION:	Five-speed manual (optional four-speed automatic)
DRIVE:	Part-time four-wheel drive; dual-range transfer box

STEERING:	Power-assisted rack and pinion
BRAKES:	Front discs; self-adjusting rear drums; servo assisted
SUSPENSION:	Five-link rigid with coil springs and MacPherson struts
OVERALL LENGTH:	3,860mm
OVERALL WIDTH:	1,695mm
OVERALL HEIGHT:	1,675–1,690mm
WHEELBASE:	2,200mm
GROUND CLEARANCE:	195mm

Suzuki GV2000

ENGINE:	1,995cc 16-valve DOHC four-cylinder; multi-point fuel-injection
MAX POWER:	126bhp @ 6,000rpm
MAX TORQUE:	128.3lb ft @ 2,900rpm
PERFORMANCE:	Max speed 96mph
ECONOMY:	Approx. 30mpg
TRANSMISSION:	Five-speed manual (optional four-speed automatic)
DRIVE:	Part-time four-wheel drive; dual-range transfer box
STEERING:	Power-assisted rack and pinion
BRAKES:	Front discs; self-adjusting rear drums; servo assisted
SUSPENSION:	Five-link rigid with coil springs and MacPherson struts
OVERALL LENGTH:	3,870mm
OVERALL WIDTH:	1,695mm
OVERALL HEIGHT:	1,675–1,690mm
WHEELBASE:	2,200mm
GROUND CLEARANCE:	195mm

Suzuki GV2000 TD

ENGINE:	1,997cc direct-injection OHC four-cylinder diesel with intercooler
MAX POWER:	107bhp @ 6,000rpm
MAX TORQUE:	199lb ft @ 1,750rpm
PERFORMANCE:	Max speed 92mph
ECONOMY:	30.1mpg (urban); 47.1mpg (extra urban); 38.7mpg (combined)
TRANSMISSION:	Five-speed manual
DRIVE:	Part-time four-wheel drive; dual-range transfer box
STEERING:	Power-assisted rack and pinion
BRAKES:	Front discs; self-adjusting rear drums; servo assisted
SUSPENSION:	Five-link rigid with coil springs and MacPherson struts
OVERALL LENGTH:	3,870mm
OVERALL WIDTH:	1,695mm
OVERALL HEIGHT:	1,675–1,690mm

| WHEELBASE: | 2,200mm |
| GROUND CLEARANCE: | 195mm |

Suzuki Grand Vitara 2.0 16v LWB

ENGINE:	1,995cc 16-valve DOHC four-cylinder; multi-point fuel-injection
MAX POWER:	126bhp @ 6,000rpm
MAX TORQUE:	128.3lb ft @ 2,900rpm
PERFORMANCE:	Max speed 95mph
ECONOMY:	23.5mpg (urban); 36.2mpg (extra urban); 30.4mpg (combined)
TRANSMISSION:	Five-speed manual (optional four-speed automatic)
DRIVE:	Part-time four-wheel drive; dual-range transfer box
STEERING:	Power-assisted rack and pinion
BRAKES:	Front discs; self-adjusting rear drums; servo assisted
SUSPENSION:	Five-link rigid with coil springs and MacPherson struts
OVERALL LENGTH:	4,215mm
OVERALL WIDTH:	1,780mm
OVERALL HEIGHT:	1,740mm
WHEELBASE:	2,480mm
GROUND CLEARANCE:	195mm

Suzuki Grand Vitara 2.0 TD LWB

ENGINE:	1,997cc direct-injection OHC four-cylinder diesel with intercooler
MAX POWER:	107bhp @ 6,000rpm
MAX TORQUE:	199lb ft @ 1,750rpm
PERFORMANCE:	Max speed 90mph
ECONOMY:	30.1mpg (urban); 47.1mpg (extra urban); 38.7mpg (combined)
TRANSMISSION:	Five-speed manual
DRIVE:	Part-time four-wheel drive; dual-range transfer box
STEERING:	Power-assisted rack and pinion
BRAKES:	Front discs; self-adjusting rear drums; servo assisted
SUSPENSION:	Five-link rigid with coil springs and MacPherson struts
OVERALL LENGTH:	4,215mm
OVERALL WIDTH:	1,780mm
OVERALL HEIGHT:	1,740mm
WHEELBASE:	2,480mm
GROUND CLEARANCE:	195mm

Suzuki Grand Vitara 2.5 V6 LWB

| ENGINE: | 2,493cc DOHC 24-valve V6; multi-point fuel-injection |

MAX POWER:	142bhp @ 6,200rpm
MAX TORQUE:	153lb ft @ 3,500rpm
PERFORMANCE:	Max speed 100mph
ECONOMY:	21.6mpg (urban); 31mpg (extra urban); 26.6mpg (combined)
TRANSMISSION:	Five-speed manual/four-speed automatic
DRIVE:	Part-time four-wheel drive; dual-range transfer box
STEERING:	Power-assisted rack and pinion
BRAKES:	Front discs; self-adjusting rear drums; servo assisted
SUSPENSION:	Five-link rigid with coil springs and MacPherson struts
OVERALL LENGTH:	4,215mm
OVERALL WIDTH:	1,780mm
OVERALL HEIGHT:	1,740mm
WHEELBASE:	2,480mm
GROUND CLEARANCE:	195mm

Suzuki Grand Vitara XL-7 2.0 TD

ENGINE:	1,997cc direct-injection OHC four-cylinder diesel with intercooler
MAX POWER:	107bhp @ 6,000rpm
MAX TORQUE:	199lb ft @ 1,750rpm
PERFORMANCE:	Max speed 90mph
ECONOMY:	27.4mpg (urban); 42.2mpg (extra urban); 35.5mpg (combined)
TRANSMISSION:	Five-speed manual
DRIVE:	Part-time four-wheel drive; dual-range transfer box
STEERING:	Power-assisted rack and pinion

BRAKES:	Front discs; self-adjusting rear drums; servo assisted
SUSPENSION:	Five-link rigid with coil springs and MacPherson struts
OVERALL LENGTH:	4,760mm
OVERALL WIDTH:	1,780mm
OVERALL HEIGHT:	1,740mm
WHEELBASE:	2,800mm
GROUND CLEARANCE:	183mm

Suzuki Grand Vitara XL-7 2.7 V6

ENGINE:	2,736cc quad-cam 24-valve V6; multi-point fuel-injection
MAX POWER:	181bhp @ 6,000rpm
MAX TORQUE:	184.4lb ft @ 3,300rpm
PERFORMANCE:	Max speed 105mph
ECONOMY:	18.5mpg (urban); 30.4mpg (extra urban); 24.6mpg (combined)
TRANSMISSION:	Five-speed manual/four-speed automatic
DRIVE:	Part-time four-wheel drive; dual-range transfer box
STEERING:	Power-assisted rack and pinion
BRAKES:	Front discs; self-adjusting rear drums; servo assisted
SUSPENSION:	Five-link rigid with coil springs and MacPherson struts
OVERALL LENGTH:	4,760mm
OVERALL WIDTH:	1,780mm
OVERALL HEIGHT:	1,740mm
WHEELBASE:	2,800mm
GROUND CLEARANCE:	183mm

Index